Sandy Becker

Informal Learning on the Job

Victoria J. Marsick &

Marie Volpe, Editors

Advances in Developing Human Resources (ISSN 1523-4223) is a quarterly monograph series published by the Academy of Human Resource Development and Berrett-Koehler Communications, Inc.

Academy of Human Resource Development
P.O. Box 25113
Baton Rouge, LA 70894-5113

Berrett-Koehler Communications, Inc.
8 California Street, Suite 610
San Francisco, CA 94111-4825

Subscription Orders: Please send subscription orders to Berrett-Koehler Communications, PO Box 565, Williston, VT 05495, or call 800-929-2929, or fax 802-864-7626. Subscriptions cost $79 for individuals and $125 for institutions. All orders must be prepaid in U.S. dollars or charged to Visa, MasterCard, or American Express. For orders outside the United States, please add $15 for surface mail or $30 for air mail. Librarians are encouraged to write for a free sample issue. **Standing Orders:** By designating your subscription as a "Standing Order" that will remain in effect until you cancel it, you will save both yourself and Berrett-Koehler the paperwork of annual renewal notices, and you will receive a 10 percent discount from the annual subscription rate. **Multiple Copies:** Ten or more copies of a single issue of *Advances in Developing Human Resources* can be purchased at a 20 percent discount. Please contact Berrett-Koehler Communications sales department, PO Box 565, Williston, VT 05495-9900; call 800-929-2929; fax to 802-864-7626; or visit www.bkconnection.com.

Editorial Correspondence: Address editorial correspondence and inquiries to Richard A. Swanson, Editor-in-Chief, *Advances in Developing Human Resources*, University of Minnesota, 1954 Buford Avenue, Suite 425, St. Paul, MN 55108, USA. E-mail: swanson2@cris.com

Library of Congress Cataloging-in-Publication Data

Informal learning on the job / Richard A. Swanson, editor-in-chief ; Victoria J. Marsick, Marie Volpe, editors.
p. cm. — (Advances in developing human resources)
Includes index.
ISBN 1-58376-023-7 (alk. paper)
1. Employees—Training of. 2. Occupational training. 3. Experiential learning. I. Swanson, Richard A., 1942-. II. Marsick, Victoria J. III. Volpe, Marie. IV. Series.
HF5549.5.T7 I4572 1999
658.3'124–dc21 99-40909
CIP

 Printed in the United States of America on acid-free and recycled paper.

Postmaster: Please send address changes to the Berrett-Koehler address above.
Cover Design: Carolyn Deacy Design, San Francisco, CA
Production: Pleasant Run Publishing Services, Williamsburg, VA

Preface v
Marie Volpe and Victoria J. Marsick

1. **The Nature of and Need for Informal Learning** 1
Victoria J. Marsick and Marie Volpe
The authors discuss informal learning and the need for continuous learning in today's workplace. They preview the themes discussed in the other chapters and discuss implications of those themes for practice.

2. **Learning Informally in the Aftermath of Downsizing** 10
Marie Volpe
The author describes how human resources professionals learn to cope with major organizational changes. A typology using Bolman and Deal's framework for understanding organizations shows that the ways individuals make sense of their environment influence their capacity and choices as learners.

3. **Learning Partnerships** 22
Barbara Keelor (Larson) Lovin
The author explores how people learn through partnerships, focusing on partnerships between paramedics and how the nature of the challenges these partners face influences their choices and strategies for learning.

4. **Learning to Be an Effective Team Member** 33
Sally Vernon
The author explores how individuals learn about teamwork in not-for-profit organizational settings. The author identifies skills and strategies to meet the challenges of learning collaboratively in an organization.

5. **How Managers Learn in the Knowledge Era 42**
Kathleen Dechant
Managers are often the first to feel the brunt of rapid change. The author draws on two studies to show how managers learn rapidly under stressful, turbulent conditions, as well as how they draw others collaboratively into a learning network.

6. **"Awakening": Developing Learning Capacity in a Small Family Business 52**
Mary Ziegler
The author traces the strategies implemented by the owners and managers of a small business as they intentionally begin a concerted effort to become a learning organization.

7. **Critical Reflection as a Response to Organizational Disruption 66**
Ann K. Brooks
The author examines the nature and functions of critical reflection in informal learning and explores how it is supported or discouraged by the actions of managers and other conditions in the workplace environment.

8. **Theory and Practice of Informal Learning in the Knowledge Era 80**
Victoria J. Marsick, Marie Volpe, and Karen E. Watkins
The authors draw on lessons learned from the preceding chapters. They rethink their model of informal learning and implications for practice, based on insights from these studies about the nature of informal learning, learning strategies, and conditions that facilitate learning.

Appendix: Design of Studies 96
Victoria J. Marsick

Index 101
The Authors 106

Preface

Marie Volpe
Victoria J. Marsick

The heart of this issue of *Advances in Developing Human Resources* is a number of descriptions of what informal learning looks like in different work settings. All of the studies reported in this issue are descriptive and qualitative in nature and are based on interviews and observation. They use stories to help you see how people experience informal learning at work. They also uncover some of the common difficulties that arise because informal learning is frequently left to the individual to design, direct, carry out, and evaluate.

The case studies presented here were gathered within organizational settings. We have sought as much variety as possible in the type of organizations highlighted and have focused primarily on individual learning rather than the informal learning that occurs within teams or by entire organizations.

As the flow of the chapters shows, this issue looks at individual learning in successively broader social contexts, beginning with individuals learning alone and then progressing to individuals who work and learn in partnerships and finally individuals as members of teams. The last three studies—by Dechant, Ziegler, and Brooks—verge on organizational learning, or at least on the building of learning communities, because they focus on managers. Managers can act as agents of organizational inquiry. Based on early work on organizational learning by Chris Argyris and Donald Schön (1978, 1996), we concur that organizations can learn when someone inquires into challenges on behalf of the organization.

These individuals act on new knowledge to change the organization's culture, structure, practices, mental models, or other artifacts. In so doing, they typically involve others they work with in a collective learning process. These last studies illustrate how individuals shepherd that process of organizational learning through their own knowledge creation.

We expect that many readers will be more interested in the findings of these studies than in how the research was conducted. Therefore the authors have kept details of their studies to a minimum within each chapter. For those who are interested, we have included an appendix that lays out the general design for most of these qualitative case studies. We also describe the conceptual framework that was the starting point for most of these studies, even though the data often sent these researchers to other sources to help them interpret emerging findings.

Chapter Two, by Marie Volpe, is set back in the earlier days of downsizing and organizational restructuring and illustrates how individuals affected by these changes learn to cope with them. Volpe notes that before people can learn, they have to make sense of a rapidly changing environment. She taps into what Mezirow (1991) might call meaning making, which also illustrates Weick's concept (1995) of sense making. Using Bolman and Deal's frameworks (1984) for understanding the culture of organizations, Volpe develops a typology of learners. She also shows how the sense that learners make of their environment influences their capacity and choices as learners. Volpe looks at those who stayed within an organization after downsizing.

Chapters Three and Four help us to understand the interpersonal dimensions of learning through increasingly complex social interactions. In Chapter Three, Barbara Lovin explores the way people learn through partnerships. Her study focused on partnerships between emergency medical service paramedics, especially on the nature of the challenges they face and how this influences their choices and strategies for learning. Chapter Four turns to the way in which individuals learn about teamwork. The setting for Sally Vernon's study is a nonprofit organization. Although the focus is on the individual, the skills and strategies identified focus on the challenges of learning collaboratively within an organization.

The last three studies look at managerial learning. Managers are often the first to feel the brunt of rapid change. In Chapter Five, Kathleen Dechant reports on two studies, performed almost a decade apart, in which managers used self-directed learning strategies to address new challenges. She develops a model from her first study for explaining the managers' self-initiated learning process. In her second study, using that model, she shows how the information age has further transformed managerial learning from an individual venture to a collaborative effort at knowledge creation and management.

In Chapter Six, Mary Ziegler reports on the learning that managers in a family-owned publishing business undertook to bring their business into the new era of global, technology-driven competition. Ziegler describes an early phase of learning as one of "awakening" to a new mindset and way of working that is, on the one hand, intensely personal and, on the other hand, very public. Learning was personal in that if these family leaders could not themselves change, their business would not succeed in making its desired transition. In addition, as a small business, their learning was also everyone's learning. Leaders stimulated and modeled change and brought others along on their journey.

In Chapter Seven, Ann Brooks also speaks to the relationship of individual learning to the system's learning. She revisits her earlier study of critical reflection in a regional Baby Bell company that was restructured after its divestiture from AT&T. Individuals within the organization were pressed to think more critically so that the organization could be more innovative and flexible. Brooks found that such learning demands a more complex way of thinking to enable the constant movement of information and knowledge.

In Chapter Eight, we pull together lessons learned from these studies concerning how informal learning takes place. We revisit a theory of informal and incidental learning that Marsick and Watkins (1990) developed a decade ago, as well as other research on this topic. We look especially for insights for individuals who wish to better manage their own learning since they cannot depend on organizations to provide support for lifelong learning. We also identify strategies that organizations can use to better plan for informal learning and integrate it into their plans for training and development.

References

Argyris, C., & Schön, D. (1978). *Organizational learning: A theory of action perspective.* San Francisco: Jossey-Bass.

Argyris, C., & Schön, D. (1996). *Organizational learning II: Theory, method, and practice.* Reading, MA: Addison-Wesley.

Bolman, L. G., & Deal, T. E. (1984). *Modern approaches to understanding and managing organizations.* San Francisco: Jossey-Bass.

Marsick, V. J., & Watkins, K. E. (1990). *Informal and incidental learning in the workplace.* London: Routledge.

Mezirow, J. D. (1991). *Transformative dimensions of adult learning.* San Francisco: Jossey-Bass.

Weick, K. E. (1995). *Sensemaking in organizations.* Thousand Oaks, CA: Sage.

The Nature and Need for Informal Learning

Victoria J. Marsick
Marie Volpe

The Problem and the Solution. When organizations change, employees are challenged to learn continuously through both formal and informal means. Human resources developers need to know more about how to enhance such learning. Research suggests that work can be designed to make time and space for learning. People learn more when they continually scan their environment, heighten their awareness around learning, pay attention to goals and turning points, and develop skills of reflection while taking action. Finally, people learn more easily in a culture of collaboration and trust.

The ethos of organizations has changed. Over the past three decades, in response to economic pressures, over half of all Fortune 500 companies have downsized, reorganized, or otherwise reinvented themselves. As a result, most U.S. businesses today are less paternalistic and less prescriptive, and virtually all operate in a less predictable environment. Historically, formal training and education in the workplace was used to support organizational effectiveness. Formal classroom instruction, on-the-job training, and long-term experience within a relatively static system were the avenues by which management communicated how work was to be performed. Throughout the history of productive organizations, most workplace learning has been left in the hands of employees and has been gained through informal methods and through trial and error.

Given the complexity of today's competitive global marketplace, formal and informal training and education as we have come to know them are now seen as insufficient. Old ways of solving problems will not work in today's unstable, unpredictable organizational environments. Most people at the top of organizations recognize that their role is primarily strategic and that they no longer have all the answers. Those in charge now seek new ways to unleash the creativity and innovation inherent within the organization. Depending on one's perspective, people who work with organizations see these developments as great opportunities for learning or as a time of rampant exploitation, when anything goes.

Training Versus Learning

Any discussion of how learning supports organizational effectiveness must begin with an understanding of the difference between training and learning. Traditionally, training has been viewed in terms of discrete planned events (experiences) used to instruct people how to perform specific defined jobs. Learning, by contrast, is understood as an ongoing lifelong process. Senge speaks to this from an organizational perspective when he says, "Through learning we extend our capacity to create, to be part of the generative process of life" (1990, p. 14). The thesis of this issue is that learning, as opposed to training, is more appropriate to a business environment in which jobs are constantly changing.

Traditional training assumes that organizations can analyze a task, process, or function to discover an optimal means of performing it, document that optimal method, and then prescribe the required skills or expertise that a learner must master to perform that task. Learning was seen to take place only or primarily in the training room. And those responsible for training rarely focused on the need for post-training support. After studying the impact of technology on learning in a variety of organizations, Shoshana Zuboff (1988) concluded that intelligent technology can enable an "informated" workplace, as opposed to one that is mindlessly automated. She speaks to the need to restructure jobs and organizations to encourage learning to take place on the job, in real time, through real work: "Learning is not something that requires time out from being engaged in productive activity; learning is the heart of productive activity. To put it simply, learning is the new form of labor" (p. 395). But to effect this shift, managers must make the right choices—choices that will enable people and organizations to fulfill the promise of new ways of learning.

Formal Versus Informal Learning

Today, more and more organizations are beginning to focus on fostering informal learning. Increasingly, organizations are regarding formal training programs as only one learning tool and are acknowledging that informal learning has always been the most pervasive type of learning in the workplace. We believe that, alongside this recognition, organizations need to purposefully provide a working environment that promotes and encourages opportunities for continual informal learning. Organizations need to help people make more informed decisions about what they are going to learn and help them see how their own goals mesh with those of the organization. There needs to be an array of well-thought-out opportunities that suit individual employees' learning styles that they can take advantage of to meet their needs. When organizations make available to employees the means to pull information and knowledge into the workplace at the exact time they need it, learners can potentially gain control of their own learning. Learning is then maximized throughout the organization and can be used to improve the capability of less experienced, less knowledgeable employees to enhance overall organizational effectiveness.

Although there is a great deal of focus on the need to promote continuous informal learning in the contemporary workplace, we know little about how it can best be supported, encouraged, and developed. Thus if there is to be a formal approach to supporting informal learning, it is important to discover how informal learning actually works.

To this end, several research studies have been conducted over the last decade on the role of informal learning in the workplace; however, to date no attempts have been made to assess their findings. The purpose of this issue is to provide trainers and human resources professionals with six recent studies and a synthesis of their findings, to aid them in helping organizations better support informal learning in the workplace. The following section provides an overview of what we have learned about informal learning through the research described in the following chapters.

What These Studies Show About Informal Learning

About a decade ago, Marsick and Watkins (1990) set out to describe and define informal learning. The theoretical framework they developed is examined in Chapter Eight in light of what has been learned about the dynamics of informal learning from the studies presented in Chapters Two through Seven. In this chapter we share a working definition of informal learning and highlight common themes from the studies reported here.

Informal learning can be described as learning that is predominantly unstructured, experiential, and noninstitutional. Informal learning takes place as people go about their daily activities at work or in other spheres of life. It is driven by people's choices, preferences, and intentions. When informal learning takes place in relation to jobs, the Center for Workforce Development says, "the learning process is not determined by the organization" (1998, p. 35). The center distinguishes between the goals and process of learning. Organizations may help individuals identify a goal for learning but leave the process up to the individual. The center lists a variety of activities through which informal workplace learning occurs: "teaming, meetings, customer interactions, supervision, mentoring, shift change, peer-to-peer communication, cross-training, exploration, on-the-job training, documentation, execution of one's job, site visits" (p. 53).

Informal workplace learning is often defined in terms of a series of on-the-job activities—the action containers, if you will, for such learning. But this kind of definition covers only the surface of learning—what people see when they watch someone else learn. It is the analog to descriptions of formal training that are couched in terms of the content or methods used in training as opposed to the learning processes or experience of the student. The studies in this book include some of this kind of description, but they also seek to shed light on the essence of the informal learning process and how it is or is not supported by organizational actions, structures, processes, practices, and cultures. The case studies in this book are exploratory and descriptive in nature. Yet based on them and our other reading and experience, we here lay out several key conclusions about the nature of informal learning and what this implies for how it can be enhanced. Table 1.1 summarizes our conclusions, which we then elaborate in the following paragraphs.

First, informal learning in organizations is integrated into people's daily work and routines. Its value comes from the fact that it occurs "just in time," as people face a challenge, problem, or unanticipated need. By its nature, such learning cannot be fully preprogrammed. It arises spontaneously within the context of real work. That means that people have

Table 1.1 What We Have Learned About Informal Learning

Informal Learning	*What Enhances or Improves Learning*
• Is integrated with work and daily routines	Making time and space for learning
• Is triggered by an internal or external jolt	Scan of external and internal environment
• Is not highly conscious	Heightened consciousness or awareness
• Is haphazard and influenced by chance	Attention to goals and turning points
• Is an inductive process of reflection and action	Inductive mindset and reflective skills
• Is linked to learning of others	Dependent on collaboration and trust

to have the freedom to follow interests as they arise (although, of course, their interests will likely be guided by job-related goals). All informal learning paths will not necessarily lead to predetermined outcomes. Organizations must be willing to encourage and reward curiosity and experimentation (although for the most part businesses will always be most interested in learning that produces productivity gains). Organizations also have to design jobs, work practices, and work relationships in such a way that people can talk with one another, collaboratively solve problems, and generally seek responses to challenges that they have identified, even if this does not fit into a preset work schedule.

Second, when informal learning is enhanced, it usually begins with an internal or external jolt. Sometimes that jolt comes from the external environment—a lost or changed job or relationship, the demands of new technology, changes in the scope of one's work or responsibility, or evidence of likely failure in the absence of corrective action. Sometimes that awareness is driven internally, by a person's capacity to envision the future or to otherwise reappraise his or her focus and direction. Sometimes learning is anticipatory, occurring because a person wants to prepare for a future event by rehearsing, role-playing, or otherwise previewing the experience.

Informal learning in an organization is catalyzed by frequent scans of the environment, both by the individuals within the organization and by the organization as a whole. For individuals, this means frequently reassessing their personal vision and interests as well as assessing changes in their industry, organization, and job assignment. For organizations, leaders must, at a minimum, remain ahead of the game and identify these changes for others. Too often, many organizations find it easier to change through hindsight when they have experienced some kind of "burning platform." By contrast, leaders need to look ahead so that they are not taken by surprise when change happens. They must seek to initiate change before they sink to the bottom of the change curve. Jolts heighten awareness; heightened awareness, in turn, typically leads to reassessing the situation, which may lead to new learning to inform action. However, just because a person or organization becomes aware of a need for change does not mean that the person or organization will systematically analyze the situation or accurately identify what should be learned to satisfy that need (or how it should be learned). And just because they act, it does not mean that they will realize the full potential of their learning.

The challenge of maximizing the effectiveness of informal learning is made more difficult by the fact that much of it is not highly conscious, as the studies in this issue show. Most informal learning is tacit, taken for granted, and accomplished through social modeling, as Bandura (1986) noted (in other words, people watch other people and copy them). People also innovate in response to new challenges, and often they do so without paying much attention to how they have adapted to meet new needs. In fact, when asked, it is extremely difficult for many people to explain what they have learned or even to affirm that they have in fact learned something. People often say they learn by trial and error, but they cannot easily describe the specific situations that lead them to make this conclusion.

When people are successful at what they do, they might be drawing on informal learning of this unconscious form. Making tacit knowledge conscious, or explicit, could make them self-conscious and thus temporarily affect their effectiveness. Experts often cannot name what it is they do that makes them expert, even though others can study what they do and extract some of the pearls of their wisdom. As Nonaka and Takeuchi (1995) point out, however, organizations do need to find out what people learn informally so that they can more strategically capitalize on this learning. When an organization can explicate what people have learned informally, often through the people's own trial and error, principles and models can be made explicit, tested for applicability to other circumstances, and shared with others. Often, following analyses of protocols and expert systems, the expertise developed through the best of informal learning becomes the basis of formal training programs.

Informal learning often occurs in a haphazard fashion. It is a very human endeavor, and thus it is often idiosyncratic. Informal learning can include some structured planning or learning, but more often it is driven by serendipity. This is true even when it is driven by a focused goal or intent, such as when ones surfs the Net for information. The path of informal learning often depends on chance encounters and random events and circumstances. Only afterward do people construct a logical story to explain their learning to themselves and others.

Informal learning is enhanced when people's chances for meeting new people and ideas are increased. Although today's rapidly changing organizational environment can be confusing, it also enables people with a sense of direction to take advantage of increased encounters with new people, new challenges, and new experiences. It is also enhanced by periodic reviews, in which learners can pay explicit attention to their goals and to turning points along the way of their learning journey. These reviews help people become strategic about what they want to accomplish. People seldom plan each step of their informal learning, but by taking time to check and modify their direction against the changing landscape of their needs and goals, people can make better choices when random opportunities cross their paths.

The informal learning described in all of these studies can be viewed as an iterative process of action and reflection. On the one hand, we know a lot about the process of reflection. It involves looking back on what we have done, measuring it against what we wanted to achieve, and assessing the consequences. It might involve returning to the values and assumptions that framed our understanding of the challenge or problem in the first place and asking whether our perceptions were accurate and our values truly serve ourselves, others, or the organization. On the other hand, although we know about reflection as a concept, it is extremely hard to describe in practice. It looks different for different people; indeed, it is hard to see at all because it is internal. People reflect (or do not do so) without fanfare or warning. Therein, perhaps, lies a key difficulty in attempts to enhance or facilitate informal learning. Reflection is hard to recognize or harness. Organizations often try to improve the reflective process by formalizing it, but in so doing, they alter and sometimes mar the process, as is the case with mentoring or other strategies whose efficacy depends on spontaneity, self-selection, or self-interest. Action, by contrast, is easier to manage. As these studies show, by changing action one can often stimulate new insight, knowledge, and behaviors. However, when action occurs without reflection, it is much harder for people to make the connections they need for themselves that will lead to internal commitment and full understanding or skill acquisition.

Achieving this higher level of commitment involves careful examination of actions and their consequences. This process of being critically reflective can lead individuals to radically change how they view their world, their relationships with others, and themselves. For the individual, it involves articulating and questioning long-held assumptions and mental models of reality that have informed one's actions over time. For an organization, it involves questioning values and norms, particularly those that inhibit learning by identifying certain issues and behaviors as not being open to discussion. In this way, critical reflection becomes concerned with the organization's unseen or concealed ways of being and doing. Through critical reflection, both the individual and the organization become involved in higher-order learning. The organization becomes a learning system that allows individual members to put their new wisdom, knowledge, and skills into practice.

In this ideal context, individual employees take responsibility for their own learning. As self-directed learners (Candy, 1991), they do not rely on others to tell them what they need to learn, and they no longer rely on structured training for their learning.

Another theme that runs through these case studies is that informal learning depends on an inductive mindset and learning skills. An organization that formally recognizes the power of informal learning is more likely than one that does not to orient people to what it wants—to its strategic intent—and then to ask people to be proactive in making decisions about implementation. There are fewer managers in the workplace today to give detailed instructions, monitor outcomes, or even check with people about their progress. Yet for years employees have relied on their organizations to set the boundaries of what they need to know. Thus effective informal learning requires a mindset and skills that employees might not have. People in the workplace need to construct their own lessons, and to do this they need skill at gathering data, assembling evidence, checking their reasoning, and asking others to check their conclusions. Learning takes place in action. A key to good learning is often the capacity to ask good questions that might well lead to reframing the problem or deciding on totally different directions.

Finally, although these studies focus on how individuals learn in organizations, it is clear that informal learning in today's workplace is not a solitary venture. Increasingly, people are being asked to work closely with others throughout their organization to develop creative new solutions to business challenges. They are also being rewarded, in part, for sharing and for teamwork. People tend to believe that others perceive things as they do. But people's understanding is highly influenced by their history and experience, and employees might find that they are using the same words but not talking in the same language. There is little time to sort out this confusion, yet success depends on listening to one another, checking for understanding, ensuring that people are "on the same page," and negotiating around conflicts and differences of opinion. A key prerequisite of successful collaborative learning is a collaborative work environment. Resoundingly, these studies point to the importance of creating environments of basic trust in which people know that asking a question or making a mistake will not be misunderstood or punished.

References

Argyris, C., & Schön, D. (1978). *Organizational learning: A theory of action perspective.* San Francisco: Jossey-Bass.

Bandura, A. (1986). *Social foundations of thought and action: A social cognitive theory.* Englewood Cliffs, NJ: Prentice-Hall.

Candy, P. C. (1991). *Self-direction for lifelong learning: A comprehensive guide to theory and practice.* San Francisco: Jossey-Bass.

Center for Workforce Development. (1998). *The teaching firm: Where productive work and learning converge.* Report on research findings and implications. Newton, MA: Education Development Center, Inc.

Marsick, V. J., & Watkins, K. E. (1990). *Informal and incidental learning in the workplace.* London: Routledge.

Nonaka, I., & Takeuchi, H. (1995). *The knowledge-creating company.* New York: Oxford.

Senge, P. M. (1990). *The fifth discipline: The art and practice of the learning organization.* New York: Doubleday.

Zuboff, S. (1988). *In the age of the smart machine: The future of work and power.* New York: Basic Books.

Learning Informally in the Aftermath of Downsizing

Marie Volpe

The Problem and the Solution. The rash of downsizing that occurred in the eighties and nineties posed significant challenges for human resources professionals, who were charged with helping employees adjust to a very different set of rules even as they had to modify their own outlook. The author identifies three groups with different needs for learning and adjustment in the downsized environment: the self-defined, the heartbroken, and the survivalists. Each group has different learning needs, but all need to become more aware of the need for learning continuously on the job to solve complex problems in innovative ways.

The American business environment has changed dramatically over the last thirty years. Many of the factors that have contributed to those changes are interrelated and highly complex and have had a rippling effect within organizations. Since the 1970s there have been myriad responses by organizations to the rapidly and continuously changing business environment. Among the most common responses has been to cut costs by restructuring and downsizing. The effects of restructuring and downsizing on employees and the ways employees have responded and adapted to the changing workplace are interrelated and equally complex.

Consider, for example, the voices of these people:

- John, a high-level manager of a very large international company, views the downsized environment as highly political. As a consequence, his approach to carrying out his work has changed: "It's a political arena now, and you have to be careful. Nobody is really sure who the players are, so you're not really sure who's who, who has the political clout and who doesn't. So, it's more important now to be sure who is on your side before you bring something forward."

- Nancy, a colleague, spoke about the effects of the changed environment more in terms of loss: "The loss of loyalty between the organization and the employee is more than just a job security issue: I think it has had a real effect on productivity. Although downsizings are a part of what's happening in American businesses, I'm not at all sure they are managed well—not only while they are going on but afterward. That means I don't work long hours, I don't get my stomach knotted up when things aren't going right—I just move the problem to somebody else."
- Another high-level manager, Bob, spoke more personally about the new impersonal organization: "Remember the good old days, when we really cared about people and the issues at work were the people issues? We do far less of that now. Every study you do is a cost study. How do we lower costs? Look at this latest benefit we just issued. It's a company benefit—it's a benefit to the company, not to the employees. Now there is a little bit of give to the employees, but it's a huge benefit for the company."

These voices are illustrative of the human drama I witnessed in a company I had been a part of for many years. I watched as a rippling series of cutbacks that began small in 1982 surged and culminated in a large and very extensive downsizing in 1986. The effects of the final downsizing were further compounded by a change in the company's leadership and a major reorganization. Because of the magnitude of these dramatic events, I felt compelled to investigate how people had reacted to them and how they would learn to survive and even thrive in a very new and different organizational culture. Thus I began a study of informal learning sparked by major organizational change.

During 1986, three major changes took place almost simultaneously within the company:

1. The company initiated a massive 25 percent reduction of its worldwide workforce.
2. Concurrent with the downsizing program, the company embarked on an extensive restructuring of all of its worldwide operations.

3. Both a new chairman and a new president were elected to lead the company.

The company that emerged from these changes in 1987 was almost a stranger to those who had worked in and known the company for many years. Deep and profound changes had ruptured the old organization, and a new and unfamiliar one had appeared. The differences in the company caused by these changes are summarized in Table 2.1.

One of the company's most significant characteristics in its downsized state is instability. Instead of maintaining a steady state, the company is now constantly in flux, like a vehicle that moves at varying rates of speed in response to a dynamic, always-changing, unpredictable external environment. This instability poses significant challenges for all of the company's employees in terms of learning to perform one's job in a less predictable environment, finding meaning in one's work, and maintaining one's self-esteem.

The Study

The Subjects

I decided to focus my study on the company's human resource (HR) professionals, for two reasons. First, I assumed that because of the nature of their work, there would be a correlation between HR professionals' ability to adapt to change and their ability to effectively respond to the needs of their clients—both management and employees—in the new environment. Second, I further assumed that the extent to which HR professionals were able to learn what they needed to know to survive, if not thrive, in the changing organization would be related to their ability to help and influence the learning of others.

Assumptions

The study was also based on these important assumptions: that most learning in the workplace occurs in informal and nonstructured situations, that the need for continuous informal learning increases during periods of intense organizational change, and that an implied social contract existed between the organization and its employees before downsizing occurred.

Table 2.1 Business Models Before and After Downsizing

Before Downsizing	*After Downsizing*
Stability and steady growth	Instability and rapid change
Hierarchical/bureaucratic and authority based	Hierarchical/bureaucratic and some move toward interdependency
Focus on procedures and mechanisms of control	Focus on business needs and customer requirements
One boss: manager	Many bosses: managers/customers
Job security/lifetime career with company	Job insecurity/possible career continuation outside company
Rapid vertical advancement every few years	Gradual vertical or horizontal career moves
Depth and specialization of skills	Breadth and integration of skills
Roles and responsibilities compartmentalized	Roles and responsibilities interdependent/flexible

Research Base

Kurt Lewin's theory (1935) that behavior is a function of the interactions between a person and his or her environment provided the overriding construct for this analysis and synthesis of the research findings. Bolman and Deal's four-frame approach to analyzing organizations (1984) was used to assess the extent and nature of the environmental changes confronting the HR professionals participating in the study.

Key Issues

Although this study set out to examine how a group of HR professionals learned to master change, a key finding was that the overriding issue for them was the need to understand the changed environment. This issue hindered their learning in informal situations as well as their ability to meet their clients' needs.

Furthermore, the study identified three common perceptions among workers in the downsized environment: that the nature of work has changed, that the company is no longer a paternal organization, and that the organizational environment has become highly complex politically. The following sections look more closely at these key findings.

Across the board, the people in the study indicated that the 1986 restructuring and downsizing had had significant implications for them, their work, and the way in which they viewed their relationship with the company. The old unifying culture and traditions, which had tended to foster dependency on the organization and had featured explicit, externally defined rules and guidelines, had given way to a hodgepodge of differing perspectives. In addition, the way the company's HR professionals perceived the downsized environment also affected *what they learned*, and their perceptions of what the company's employees needed to learn to master the new environment appeared to be related to *how they learned informally*.

Three Perspectives

Three of Bolman and Deal's frames (1984)—the structural frame, the human resources frame, and the political frame—provide a method for clustering three generally discernible perspectives among employees regarding what they need to learn in a downsized environment. I call the three groups characterized by these different perspectives the self-defined, the heartbroken, and the survivalists.

The Self-Defined

Although the HR professionals who held this perspective were a minority (20 percent of the participant population), as a group they appeared to hold a balanced view of the downsized environment. Their view was that the nature of how work was to be done had changed and that therefore they needed to figure out how to get their work done, learn the new standards to apply to work, and how to sort out and make sense of the new roles, responsibilities, and relationships that had arisen inside the company following the many personnel moves accompanying the reorganization and downsizing.

This group expressed confidence in their competencies and spoke of the possibility of their pursuing career options and choices beyond the company if they were to deem it in their best interest. In addition, although they indicated that their work was very important to them, they were the only participants who discussed the importance of having balance in life. They spoke of pursuing outside activities that contribute to their being "self-defined," rather than accepting the company's definition of who they are.

The Heartbroken

The HR professionals who held this perspective (35 percent of the participant population) stressed that the company's culture had changed dramatically. They perceived the reorganization and downsizing and the new leadership's distance from the workforce as evidence that the company no longer cared about its employees. This "heartbroken" group appeared to be the most disoriented by the changes that took place in 1986. They believed the company had broken an unwritten contract with its employees, and consequently they felt disillusioned, disappointed, and betrayed.

These individuals appeared to be less self-defined than the first group. They expressed a strong identification with the pre-1986 company, stating that their values had been strongly aligned with what they had believed the company stood for and valued. They described their subsequent distrust of the company and loss of loyalty to it following the 1986 downsizing. From their perspective, what they most needed to learn to function in the new organizational environment was how to handle the new corporate world of shifting loyalties. To do this, they would need to develop an inward focus and reassess their relationship with the company. They would need to develop emotional and psychological independence to be able to manage their careers and take more control of their lives.

The Survivalists

This perspective was the most common (held by 45 percent of the participant population). The HR professionals in this group tended to view the downsized environment neither more nor less positively than they had viewed the previous environment. They simply saw the downsized environment as a new reality in which one has to compete for scarce resources to survive and advance.

This group avowed that the technical and interpersonal skills that had been required for success in the company prior to 1986 were still sufficient to maintain one's professional status and even to advance in the downsized company. What is now needed in addition to those skills, they asserted, is heightened political skills. This, they explained, involves understanding where emerging new power bases are and knowing how to satisfy various interest groups within the company, even if it means holding back information or telling the boss what he or she wants to hear at all costs.

As the preceding discussion makes clear, the primary order of business for all of the HR professionals in the study was to understand the new downsized organizational environment and their place within it. Because the participants had different perceptions of the new environment, however, what they learned or believed they needed to learn differed across the three groups.

Based on their differing perspectives of the downsized environment, each of the groups had different learning goals. These goals are described in Figure 2.1.

The Breakdown of Informal Learning

In the downsized company, employees learned by means of independent strategies rather than learning informally by interacting with others, the more common practice before the downsizing. The following paragraphs describe some of the reasons why there were fewer opportunities to learn informally through others after 1986.

Loss of Informal Networks

First, there was a breakdown of the informal networks within the company. Before 1986, informal networking among colleagues in work groups and across affiliates was common. In the downsized environment, by contrast, there was far less trust between people in the organization. This was stressed especially by those who perceived the environment as more political than in the past (the survivalists). This group, in particular, closed ranks and became reluctant to share information with others.

The group who believed that they could no longer trust the company or many of its members (the heartbroken group) also closed ranks by shar-

Figure 2.1 Goals of the Three Types of Learners

- The ***self-defined*** group's goals were to
  1. Identify the new roles, responsibilities, and relationships within the reorganized environment
  2. Develop transportable skills in addition to the bureaucratic company-specific skills they had developed in the past

- The ***heartbroken*** group's goals were to
  1. Develop emotional and psychological independence to gain control over their career and life
  2. Learn ways to strengthen their self-esteem to develop a sense of having options and balance
  3. Develop a personal identity not tied to the company
  4. Reexamine previous belief in lifelong career and job security

- The ***survivalist*** group's goals were to
  1. Identify where the new power bases are
  2. Understand how to satisfy multiple complex interests
  3. Determine how to get scarce resources from those in power
  4. Figure out how to protect their manager/supervisor, to protect themselves

ing their disappointment with select others who held a similar view. As a consequence, the self-defined group, who primarily focused on their work, did not feel betrayed by the company, and did not perceive the environment as more political than before, had fewer opportunities to learn through informal networks. Simply stated, the survivalists weren't going to share information, and the heartbroken group was so introspective that its members had nothing to share.

Loss of Formal Networks

There was also a loss of formal networks of experts and specialists following 1986. These previously organized networks had been highly regarded for their members' knowledge and technical skills, which had developed over time. When many of these individuals left as a result of the downsizing, loss of their expertise caused a "brain drain" in the organization.

Those who remained found it difficult to get the expert advice and counsel they needed. Thus there was more "reinventing the wheel," and there were fewer opportunities—formal *or* informal—to learn from the experience and expertise of others.

Loss of Formal and Informal Mechanisms for Learning

Before the downsizing, the company had formally established mechanisms that provided valuable informal learning resources. For example, there were regular brown-bag lunches on current HR issues. There was also the "College of Benefits Knowledge," an informal series of training sessions held after work hours by experienced HR benefits experts who volunteered to help inform and instruct other HR professionals. And there were similar informal instructional and information-sharing meetings routinely moderated by other HR functions, such as compensation and labor relations. After downsizing, these informal learning opportunities all but disappeared.

Loss of Mentors and Coaches

Many of the individuals separated from the company had served as coaches, role models, and mentors and as such had been great sources of informal learning in the company prior to the downsizing. Before 1986, most employees had regarded their managers and supervisors as coaches and guides with respect to how to perform their work, how to perfect their presentation style, and how to advance their careers. After 1986, subordinates no longer viewed their managers and supervisors as facilitators of this kind of informal learning.

Increase in Stress

The study participants described the postdownsizing transitional environment as very stressful. The reductions in staff meant that fewer people were doing more work. One participant, commenting on the sheer volume of work, said, "with all the work, there is no time to train or be trained—no time to learn." Stress from overwork was compounded by confusion brought on by the reorganization and, for some, anxiety and insecurity about the potential for more downsizing or, for others, the loss of paternalism within the organization. The study participants appeared to have varying ability to cope with these stresses; for some they were more debilitating than they were for others. Thus learning in the downsized company was impeded to the extent that individual employees were preoccupied with the pressures of an exceedingly stressful environment.

Formal networks of experts and strong informal networks of peers and colleagues had been the primary venues for informal learning in the predownsized company. After the downsizing, learning through others in the workplace was seriously impeded by several factors. Many of the company historians and experts who had composed the formal networks had left. Because of differing perspectives, the downsized environment was less conducive to informal networking and hence to informal learning. Finally, there were a smaller number of people doing more work in a highly stressful environment, which left less time for informal sharing of information and learning.

The New Game

The major finding of this study is that the sample group of HR professionals did not master change. They could not get in touch with this task because their first and overriding order of business was to understand the new downsized organizational culture. The changes that took place within the company in 1986 created a totally different learning environment than what had existed there before. The pre–1986 culture and traditions, which had encouraged dependence on long-established, well-defined rules and guidelines, had given way to a more ambiguous organizational environment. Therefore, HR professionals had to learn the emerging new organizational values and norms, determine what standards to follow in carrying out their work, and redefine their relationship with the company. They had to learn the new rules of the game, first to survive and later to maintain their status or even advance in the downsized environment.

Lessons Learned

Organizations implementing major changes cannot predict one common response from their employees. Companies undergoing such change must align their organizational systems and development processes to support three distinct learning needs among their employees: the need to learn how to accomplish tasks in the new environment, the need to identify and understand new cultural norms and organizational values, and the need for personal and professional development.

It is especially critical to satisfy these different learning needs among HR professionals. Since the study participants' learning goals following the downsizing focused primarily on their own survival, they were less likely or able to help others in the organization learn to cope with the change. In most organizations, HR professionals are in contact with a broad range of employees. Playing a dual role, they provide advice and counsel to both line management and employees on company programs, policies, and procedures. They are also seen as a resource for employees on issues pertaining to inequities or unfair treatment. They represent management by communicating the company's philosophy, policies, and programs to employees and by handling a wide range of people-related issues. Since they are on the frontline of employee-company relations, their perceptions of the organizational environment, of management, and of their own professional competencies influence their ability to serve their clients. In light of these responsibilities, HR professionals have the potential to affect significantly the way in which learning occurs within the organization.

Looking Forward

Although this study was conducted over ten years ago, most of the findings are still relevant today, given the persistent cycle of change characteristic of the modern workplace. There may be fewer heartbroken individuals in organizations today, but there are probably significantly more people who perceive the workplace as politically charged. Organizations need to find ways to reestablish rapport and rebuild trust with those individuals, by increasing and opening up communication with those who remain in the transformed environment.

Decision makers in organizations undergoing major change should consider establishing a new commitment to their employees. This does not mean reinventing the past—it means examining past practices and reinstituting those that were effective. It means reviving brown-bag lunches and informal after-hours training of the type described previously. Organizations should encourage and support these kinds of informal exchanges and provide the time and resources needed to conduct them.

Additionally, organizations should provide opportunities that facilitate on-the-job informal learning. This begins by creating awareness of the need for new learning as a continuous process on the job, one that leads employees to solve complex problems in innovative and creative ways. Facilitating on-the-job informal learning also involves changing old attitudes that are no longer appropriate and encouraging new ones (for example, recognizing the value of reading a book at one's desk, fostering learning through new teamwork designs, and encouraging all employees to challenge their assumptions and beliefs about traditional ways of approaching and carrying out work). In sum, in the new business environment the organization—through its managers and supervisors—must identify the competencies required for organizations to be competitive and employees to be valued in the twenty-first century.

References

Bolman, L. G., & Deal, T. E. (1984). *Modern approaches to understanding and managing organizations.* San Francisco: Jossey-Bass.

Lewin, K. (1935). *A dynamic theory of personality.* New York: McGraw-Hill.

Chapter 3

Learning Partnerships

Barbara Keelor (Larson) Lovin

The Problem and the Solution. Those who work in partnerships face special challenges. This chapter examines partnerships between paramedics to explore the different kinds of partnerships that exist in the working world because either the work itself or the relationship itself is routine or nonroutine. Additive, potentiated, and synergistic partnerships have implications for staffing and learning in an organization.

The paramedics who staff this nation's ambulances work mostly in pairs—as partners, with equal credentials if not necessarily equal experience. Their job assignment, although it is often viewed from the outside as "to save lives," is in fact to jointly take control of a continuing series of discrete events when they respond to calls for emergency care.

Let's begin with the assumption that all paramedics have equal qualifications. All are certified by an officially recognized agency to provide medical care for patients outside the hospital. So, what happens when two paramedics must complete a task together? The answer to this question lies in the type of partnership that exists between paramedics. Within that partnership is the potential for learning, for partnerships can serve as a stimulus to learning and also as a learning tool.

Not all partnerships between paramedics are equal because the effectiveness of each pair is different when they work with familiar or unfamiliar tasks or people. The study reported in this chapter revealed four specific types of partnerships between paramedics, resulting from the various ways they were paired by their employer. Three of these are less than ideal and fail to consistently achieve the potential inherent in the partnerships. Only with the fourth type, synergistic partnership, is the true effectiveness and efficiency of the partnership structure realized. This is the type of partnership that paramedics' employers expect and demand during emergency medical situations.

The Study

The uniqueness of the working relationship between paramedic partners and the nature of their work provided the impetus for a qualitative case study of informal learning among paramedics (Larson, 1991). I conducted the study in a southeastern state, among paramedics employed by a nationwide provider of emergency medical services. I was especially interested in the informal learning that occurs within partnerships.

Twenty males and three females among the fifty-six full-time paramedics employed by the service at the time of the study participated. They had a variety of partnership experiences, resulting from being paired with other paramedics for as long as several years or as short as several hours. All experienced extended periods of contact with their partners, due to the common staffing pattern of twenty-four hours on duty followed by forty-eight hours off duty. The primary data sources were writings by each paramedic about a critical incident or challenge faced on the job, a semistructured interview with each paramedic, and observations of three of the study participants during extended work periods.

Partnership Types

The three less-than-ideal types of partnerships are the potentiated partnership, the additive partnership, and the antagonistic partnership. The optimal type is the synergistic partnership. Each is described in the following paragraphs.

Potentiated Partnerships

Typically, organizations view the potentiated partnership, in which a mentor is paired with a learner or apprentice, as providing the greatest benefit. This structure is used by the emergency services company for the same purpose as mentoring programs are used in other organizations—to introduce new employees to the system, to train current employees in how to handle difficult situations, and to foster careers. The paramedic mentors in the company do make clear their expectations for the relationship and outline plans of action for achieving the goals set out by the organization. At times the relationship works, because learners trust their mentors. Learners gain confidence from having a mentor present to back up their performance during difficult situations. The learners in the study also acknowledged that most of what they know about the organization and its expectations they learned from their mentors, and they perceived this information as accurate. This is illustrated by Dave, who said, "Basically everything I picked up about how things ran, what we could do, what we couldn't do, and what procedure was—that kind of thing—was from my partner."

In this sense the potentiated partnership structure achieves the goals set forth by the organization, and it even, at times, realizes the full potential of the partnership. However, paramedics in a potentiated partnership do not always view each other as equals. With so much at stake, mentors admit that they do not trust their partners, and it is this lack of trust that prevents the partnership from consistently achieving its potential. When the patient's condition warrants it, mentors step in and assume control, time and again. Each time this occurs the patient is being cared for by only half of the partnership. Not only might this situation affect patient care, but it also becomes a significant hindrance to learning and to the job performance of the learner, who is left to speculate as to the reasons for the mentor's actions. Although mentors may later review their actions with their partner, this can occur long after the fact, whenever there is time available in the work schedule. By this time, the subtleties of the case may have been forgotten by the mentor, and the learner may have forgotten questions that occurred to him or her during the event.

Potentiated partnerships are a common initial experience for many paramedics. They introduce new employees to the organizational culture and provide a mechanism for new paramedics to gain confidence in their patient care skills. But the potentiated partnership never lasts long enough to foster a career. There is also no evidence that the experience of mentoring or being mentored is useful as a strategy for learning how to function in a partnership.

Additive Partnerships

In an additive partnership, the effectiveness of the partners is never enhanced by their working together. Such a partnership occurs most frequently among paramedics when experienced individuals are paired for a brief time or when there are no expectations that a partnership will be permanent. Neither situation appears to act as a stimulus to learning how to function in a partnership. The partners feel that because of a real or perceived time limit on the life of the partnership, there is no benefit in putting forth the effort necessary to enhance the team's effectiveness. Tom expressed it this way: "If you saw something [your partner] wasn't doing the way you had always done it, you might not mention it. You might not be working [with that partner] for quite some time, and your one moment of saying something wouldn't change [the way he or she works]."

Individualism is characteristic of the additive partnership. The paramedics I studied who were in this type of partnership behaved as if they were working on their own. When communication occurred, it was neither consultation to reach consensus nor questioning to gain information. Rather, it took the form of the imperative, aimed only at accomplishing the task at hand. The result was simply the sum of the two paramedics' individual abilities, rather than the leveraged effectiveness expected from pairing them. Paramedics expressed dissatisfaction with this type of relationship and recognized that it invalidated the potential of the partnership structure. Jane spoke directly to this point: "I've worked with people who say, 'OK, this is your patient. I'm hands off; I'm just driving the truck, and I'll get what you need.' I'd rather they participated in patient care more." Clearly this model is not a means of moving toward a synergistic partnership.

Antagonistic Partnerships

In an antagonistic partnership, the partners actually interfere with each other. The effectiveness of the pair is less than what the two working as individuals would display. Despite the name of this structure, this situation occurs most often at the beginning of a long-term partnership in which both members are committed to developing an effective working relationship. Steve describes his experience in this kind of situation: "The paramedics speak of situations that are 'a circus' because of unfamiliarity with each other's methods of patient care. . . . They find themselves 'falling over each other' during the entire call."

An antagonistic partnership can also occur when part-time paramedics who do not know each other are paired or when partners paired for the long term fail to move beyond the early antagonistic phase of working together. In these situations partners have a hard time accepting each other as equals. A lack of trust is the significant factor in the working relationship. Lack of trust was vividly illustrated by Bill, who said, "I don't trust the other person, because I don't know what their skill capabilities are. I don't know how competent they are. I don't know how they react in a pressure situation."

Because of this lack of trust, each partner tries to take full responsibility for completing each task. Actions are not coordinated; duplication occurs. The effectiveness of the team is diminished, and the partners do not consult with each other. Obviously, an antagonistic partnership will fail to achieve the potential inherent in the situation of having two qualified paramedics work together. Yet, within this structure lies the potential for learning how to function in a partnership and a means for moving the partnership toward the effective model of a synergistic partnership.

Synergistic Partnerships

In all three of the less-than-ideal partnerships just described, the partners view their encounters with each other with mistrust. Though they are told that they are peers, their sense is that this does not describe reality. They are unsure of each other's abilities, and as a result together they often fail to meet expectations. The only partnership that meets the expectations of the organization, the public, and the partners themselves is the synergistic partnership.

Paramedics in this kind of partnership speak of acting as a single individual, communicating without words, and knowing what their partner will do before he or she does it. These long-term partners regard each other as equals. Trusting in the knowledge and experience of one's partner ultimately results in increasing his or her effectiveness. The total response to patient care is greater than the sum of the individuals' actions. This synergistic partnering is reflected in Holly's comments: "We always knew what to expect from each other all the time, no matter how unusual the situation."

Most paramedics who are or have been a member of this type of partnership are aware that it involves more than just developing the skills necessary to accomplish assigned tasks. They identify the development of the partnership as a learning process and are able to discuss the strategies they use to make this happen. The sense of mutual trust and belief that one's partner is one's equal that are characteristic of the synergistic partnership are elements that are missing from the other three types of partnerships.

Learning How to Be a Partner

Learning from experience seems to occur most often when one is faced with a unique or disconcerting event (Argyris & Schön, 1974; Barer-Stein, 1987; Marsick & Watkins, 1990). The relationships between workers can be disconcerting or the circumstances of the work itself can be disconcerting. Thus each of the four types of partnerships can be described as either routine or nonroutine.

Partnerships are routine when they are stable and nondisconcerting. They are nonroutine when they are a source of surprise, challenge, or consternation. Potentiated, additive, and antagonistic partnerships are clearly nonroutine experiences for those involved. Only a long-term, synergistic partnership is routine, and it has become so because the paramedic partners have learned to be partners.

For the individuals that make up a partnership, the experience of being paired with another person is at first a nonroutine one. *Adaptation* is the word the paramedics used to describe their process of learning to function within a partnership. In the case of paramedics, adaptation refers both to the experience of being paired with a work partner and to other facets of a job filled with nonroutine events. An experience is nonroutine for a paramedic when he or she does not have sufficient skills or knowledge to address the situation. In such situations, paramedics learn best by asking questions of themselves and others. Learning then becomes explicit. Given the appropriate circumstances, this explicit learning will be further developed during a period of experimentation. Experimentation often involves risk taking, as new interpretations are tested against previously developed skills, attitudes, behaviors, or beliefs. Experimentation can lead to rejection of the learning experience as dysfunctional or to confirmation of that experience as a path to new learning.

Partnerships Versus Tasks as Catalysts to Learning

What a paramedic partner believes he or she needs to know varies depending on the type of partnership involved. Only in the antagonistic partnership do the partners recognize a need to know how to function as a partner. Paramedics in the other two nonroutine partnerships instead concentrate on learning how to perform certain tasks. In the potentiated partnership, the focus is on job performance and meeting the expectations of the organization. For the mentor the most important thing to know is how to guide learners through the apprenticeship process. For the paramedic learner it is how to function within the organization. Once the learner performs to the mentor's satisfaction, each partner moves on to work with other individuals.

The potential for learning from and within additive partnerships is minimal. Because the individuals in an additive partnership approach their job as a series of tasks and accomplish these with a minimum of interaction, the learning that does occur is individual. The partners learn how to perform specific tasks, not how to work with each other. In additive and potentiated partnerships, paramedics fail to recognize the nonroutine experience of working with a new partner as a learning experience in and of itself. The consequence is that the potential inherent in the partnership is never achieved.

It is only in the antagonistic partnership that individuals recognize the need to learn to function as a partner. In this recognition is the potential for development of a synergistic partnership. Paramedics in most antagonistic partnerships want to consider each other as equals, want to trust each other, and want to value each other's experience. The realization of these wants occurs through the process of learning to be a partner.

Antagonistic partners learn by asking each other questions. They reflect on their assumptions about their own practice. They describe experimenting and taking risks as partners and with their partnership. As the learning develops, trust and an appreciation for each other's experience also grows. Also, the need to know how to be a partner and how to work within a partnership diminishes. The questioning ceases, only to reemerge when the team faces another nonroutine experience on the job and recognizes the need to learn how to handle it within the context of their partnership. As one partner explained, "You ask a lot of questions of each other. We still ask questions of each other when we get into predicaments." Discord concerning how to perform a task is viewed as necessary and appropriate within the partnership relationship. This is the exact opposite of what is found in potentiated and additive partnerships, where working with a partner often means accomplishing the task at hand with the least amount of discord possible.

Learning how to be a partner can take weeks or months. The learning processes that the study participants described occurred throughout this period. Confirmation that learning has occurred lies in the development of a synergistic partnership, in which the partners' knowing how to work together is tacit and their actions are spontaneous. Through the learning process the partnership moves from an antagonistic one requiring questioning, reflection, and experimentation to one of knowing-in-action. Schön (1983) describes knowing-in-action as the know-how individuals apply to the spontaneous performance of intelligent activities. He further suggests that attempts to describe such activities are always distortions of the actual performance, because the performance is dynamic but the description is static. Indeed, the study participants—aside from reporting spontaneous actions and knowing what to expect from their partners—were rarely able to explain how working within a synergistic partnership was accomplished. They recognized that they had learned to do it, but they were unable to explain how they did it. What did emerge was that the nonroutine experience of being paired with a work partner was no longer a source of surprise, challenge, or consternation. It became a routine experience of the job.

Learning Within Partnerships

It is primarily the nonroutine experiences of the job that serve as the sources of learning in this setting. There is support for the idea that what might be regarded as a nonroutine experience for individuals in one type of partnership could be routine for individuals in another type of partnership. Further, paramedics in some types of partnerships demonstrate the ability to handle nonroutine experiences as individuals. However, they might not know how to handle them as a team, or they might not wish to do so. Therefore, the potential for learning within a partnership is not only in the experience itself but also in how the experience is viewed in light of the partnership. It is here that the value of the synergistic partnership is most evident.

When faced with nonroutine experiences, synergistic partners deal with them using a process suggestive of Schön's reflection-in-action (1983). They recognize the need to solve problems, test out solutions, innovate, and invent by asking each other questions until the problem is resolved. The process is not individualistic but is engaged in by both partners in a synchronized fashion. Because the partnership is routine, the partners' responses to the nonroutine experiences encountered in the workplace are enhanced rather than encumbered by the partnership. These relationships are described in Table 3.1.

▲ Table 3.1 Responses to Job Experiences by Paramedic Partners

	Routine partnership	*Nonroutine partnership*
Routine job experience	Spontaneous	Tandem
Nonroutine job experience	Synchronous	Individual

Lessons Learned

Paramedics in nonroutine partnerships also face both routine and nonroutine job experiences. Their responses to these experiences differ significantly from those of partners in routine, or synergistic, partnerships. When the job experience is recognized as routine, the approach of individuals in all three types of nonroutine partnerships is to handle the experience in tandem. One partner assumes a leadership role, and the other follows. When the job experience is nonroutine, partners in all three types of nonroutine partnerships respond not as partners but as individuals. Mentors take over while their partners watch. Additive and antagonistic partners do what each believes should be done.

In discussing Simon's decision-making theory (1965), Marsick (Marsick and Watkins, 1990) suggests that because so much information is available, individuals have to make choices about what information they will consider. In the same manner, paramedics must make choices when faced with nonroutine tasks and nonroutine partnerships. When they are in a nonroutine partnership and are faced with a nonroutine situation, paramedics handle the predicament by acting as individuals rather than as partners. Each chooses to ignore the partnership and attend to the nonroutine task on his or her own. They move through the process as individuals, not as partners. They recognize that the effectiveness of their response, especially in urgent situations, is adversely affected by this.

When paramedics suggest that "two heads are better than one," they recognize the uniqueness of their working situation. Unfortunately, in many instances in this setting, the potential for synergistic partnership is never realized. This has significant implications for the efficient operation of emergency health care services and for effective patient care. The key to both resides in the paramedic partnership.

Looking Forward

The ability of paramedics to respond efficiently and effectively to routine and nonroutine situations depends on the existence of a synergistic partnership, with its characteristics of mutual trust and the belief that one's partner is truly one's peer. Unfortunately, the staffing practices of most emergency medical services are based on the assumption that the position of emergency caregiver can be filled at any time by any qualified paramedic familiar with the organization and its operating protocols. It is interesting to speculate what the effects would be if these organizations acknowledged that this position on the organizational chart is occupied by partnerships rather than individual paramedics. It seems clear that policies and procedures would appear that would acknowledge the importance of this working relationship, encourage consistency in staffing, and promote the concept of the partnership as one important to the organization's productivity. Paramedics certainly recognize this themselves.

One of many questions not answered by this study is whether, given the significance of partnerships, it is enough to pair individuals at random and hope that a synergistic partnership develops. The dynamics of workplace partnerships are so critical to the effectiveness of emergency medical care that it appears this issue should not be left to chance. Rather it seems incumbent on educators and trainers to facilitate formal and informal learning opportunities that emphasize the importance and dynamics of workplace relationships and ensure that individuals placed in them are adequately prepared to achieve those relationships' full potential.

References

Argyris, C., & Schön, D. A. (1974). *Theory and practice: Increasing professional effectiveness.* San Francisco: Jossey-Bass.

Barer-Stein, T. (1987). Who needs teachers? *Australian Journal of Adult Education, 27*(3), 14–26.

Larson, B. K. (1991). *Informal workplace learning and partner relationships among paramedics in the prehospital setting.* Unpublished doctoral dissertation, Columbia University.

Marsick, V. J., & Watkins, K. E. (1990). *Informal and incidental learning in the workplace.* New York: Routledge and Kegan Paul.

Schön, D. A. (1983). *The reflective practitioner: How professionals think in action.* New York: Basic Books.

Simon, H. A. (1965). *The shape of automation for men and management.* New York: Harper & Row.

Learning to Be an Effective Team Member

Sally Vernon

The Problem and the Solution. People in organizations are increasingly being asked to work in teams. It is often assumed that they can informally learn the competencies they need to be effective at working and learning in groups, but experience suggests that this is not the case. This chapter identifies structured on-the-job training as the most effective formal strategy for becoming an effective team member. It also identifies facilitators of team building and barriers to it and explores implications for practice.

One skill that has been identified as critical in meeting the challenge of the changing workplace is the ability to work as part of a team (Stephans, Mills, Pace, & Palphs, 1988). This ability is essential to successfully counter the high level of uncertainty experienced by workers faced with new technologies (Jacobs & Everett, 1988). Copeland (1988)—a researcher who focuses on diversity and multiculturalism in organizations and associated training and development activities—contends that team building is critical to managing a diverse multicultural workforce. Although education and training departments have developed numerous team-building programs to address changing human resource development needs, they have focused primarily on formal learning strategies. Yet, we know that only 10 to 20 percent of what employees learn comes from structured training (Marsick & Watkins, 1990).

The Study

This chapter explores how employees in a medium-sized, community-based, nonprofit social services agency learned informally to work more effectively in teams. The agency serves women, minorities, and others in transition by providing legal advice, social assistance, education and training, and job placement services. Like many other nonprofit agencies, it depends largely on public funding and on sources of "soft" money.

Thirty employees were interviewed, and they also wrote up critical incidents, specific descriptions concerning how they understood teaming and how they learned to become members of teams. They came from the managers' team, the public policy and development team, the managing directors' team, the administrators' team, and the clerical team. They worked in different functions and were diverse in age, ethnicity, gender, and educational background. In addition, a number of documents were analyzed for the study: institutional self-studies, planning documents, annual reports, financial records, evaluation reports, and public relations materials. Three team meetings were observed as well. The study shed light on the nature of teamwork, on strategies that are utilized to learn informally to be an effective team member, and on facilitators of and barriers to learning effective team membership.

Strategies for Learning Effective Team Membership

Structured On-the-Job Training

Participants in the study described the strategies they used to learn effective team membership. The formal learning strategies that emerged from the data included coursework, structured on-the-job training, and organizational events. A number of the study participants noted that coursework and organizational events were excellent strategies for learning work skills that enabled them to participate successfully in teams. However, structured on-the-job training—consisting of coaching, creating learning opportunities, and learning effective listening and feedback techniques—was portrayed as the most effective of these formal learning strategies. In particular, participants described access to new learning opportunities and effective feedback as critical to their growth as team members, as professionals, and as individuals. These aspects of structured on-the-job training were important to learning because they provided opportunities for employees to use informal learning strategies to add new skills to their repertoire, to affirm existing skills, and to consider how skills might apply in a variety of settings.

Informal Personal Learning Strategies

Study participants described the strategies they used, both formal and informal, to learn effective team membership. Among the informal means, personal strategies were the most frequently used. Although the study participants cited both personal and interpersonal informal strategies as helpful in learning to be an effective team member, they called the personal strategies the most beneficial to their learning process. The participants identified informal personal learning strategies as questioning, listening, observing, reading, and reflecting. Questioning, listening, reading, and observing were useful to obtain help, information, or support; to learn from alternative viewpoints; to gain the ability to provide effective feedback; and to consider alternative ways of thinking and behaving. However, only reflection allowed participants to form judgments about what was learned and to make decisions about current, future, and alternative applications of what was learned. They also used reflection to assess both the process and the outcomes of their learning experiences and of their interpersonal and trial-and-error experimentation. (Trial-and-error experimentation refers to reflecting on errors that occur because of what was done, what wasn't done, or how something was done.)

The interpersonal informal learning strategies identified by the participants were mentoring, coaching, networking, and modeling. These learning strategies have been noted in the literature as powerful informal learning tools. They were not so regarded by the participants in this study, however. The study participants' references to these learning strategies were less frequent than their references to the informal personal learning strategies. In fact, their descriptions of interpersonal informal learning strategies indicated a perception that the major purpose of networking, coaching, and modeling was to provide access to instructional materials or resources—that is, people, materials, and events—to help them in the learning process. Given this perspective, it is not surprising that the study participants cited modeling and networking as the most beneficial aspect of the interpersonal learning process. Networking was most frequently described in relation to the value of questioning as a learning device. Through networking, participants were able to ask questions that were meaningful to them and to obtain help, information, or support regarding effective team membership. Similarly, access to models provided an opportunity to observe alternative ways of behaving. The reflective dimension of learner-centered, learner-initiated learning strategies solidified the learning that occurred among the participants.

Facilitators of Learning Effective Team Membership

The study participants identified what facilitates an individual's learning how to be an effective member of a team. They also described behaviors that were indicative of these facilitators. The facilitators they described were effective leadership, effective facilitation, the interrelational aspects of teams, and individual characteristics and capabilities.

Effective Leadership

The role of team leaders was characterized by the study participants as one of establishing the parameters of the team. The purpose and philosophy of the team as well as certain structural aspects of the team must be specified or negotiated by team leaders if members are to participate fully in team activities and benefit from the learning opportunities presented by team development. The implications of these characteristics for the practice of team leaders include the need to

- Demonstrate to team members the team's value to the organization
- Develop, in tandem with team members, the purpose of the team, or articulate its purpose to team members if it has already been determined
- State the expected tenure of the team—that is, whether it will be ongoing or exist for a limited time
- Discuss the relationship between the team's purpose and the organization's overall goals and objective
- Discuss the relationship between the team's purpose and the activities of other units in the organization
- Communicate the rationale for selection of team members—that is, the expertise that was needed to achieve the purpose of the team and the size of the team in relation to its purpose
- Identify resources within the organization that will support or serve as a resource to the team
- Delineate the degree of autonomy that the team will have in making decisions, implementing innovations, initiating training activities, and assessing the team's ongoing effectiveness

- Determine an action plan, in tandem with team members, that capitalizes on the expertise of individuals and the group
- Identify, in tandem with team members, learning needs that the team may encounter
- Design, in tandem with team members, a process for ongoing assessment of team effectiveness
- Provide rewards for team process and product achievements and for continuous learning

Effective Facilitation

The study participants defined effective facilitation as providing an operational structure that ensures efficient team activity. The implications for practice of the need for an efficient operational structure include the necessity of providing or developing the following:

- Meetings that include a clear agenda and informed, prepared participants
- Relevant materials and effective time-management practices
- Access to resources, both human and material, that foster achievement of team goals and objectives
- An action plan that is jointly developed and acknowledged by team members
- Full and appropriate use and acknowledgment of the expertise of team members
- Ongoing assessment regarding the efficiency of team operations

Interrelational Facilitators

The interrelational facilitators of effective team membership identified by the study participants were practices, based on theories of group and human dynamics, that promote participation and maximum productivity from team members. Implications for practice of the need for these facilitators include fostering a team focus on

- Developing and actualizing attitudes, values, and beliefs supportive of individual and group expertise and importance
- Designing a continuous learning process to develop skills in effective communication and maximizing
- Encouraging and respecting diversity of opinion and expertise
- Integrating an ongoing assessment process into all team activities

Individual Facilitators

The study participants identified a propensity for teamwork, high self-esteem, and the perception that one is an asset to one's team as individual characteristics that facilitate the learning of effective team membership. The implications for practice of these individual facilitators are the need to

- Foster dialogue about individual and group perceptions of teamwork as a management strategy
- Establish individual and group responsibilities in response to individual perceptions of teamwork as a management strategy
- Design and implement a reward system and feedback loop that promotes individual and team development
- Integrate an ongoing process to assess environmental facilitators of positive self-esteem
- Encourage the perception that the team is effective and valuable

Barriers to Learning Effective Team Membership

The study participants placed heavy emphasis on insufficient resources, disparaging attitudes and beliefs about teamwork, and external barriers as impediments to effective team membership. They considered the resources for team membership made available by the agency—time, management support, staffing and funding, and expertise—to be insufficient. Counterproductive features of the teams themselves included the fact that membership on them was involuntary; the deprecating attitude of some team members toward teamwork; the personal styles of some team members, which conflicted with teamwork; excessive self-interest among some team members; and team politics.

Lessons Learned

The implications of this data for improving practice in facilitating workplace learning are noteworthy. First and foremost, human resource development professionals benefit from learner perceptions that systematic informal personal learning strategies are effective. This, along with environments and activities that maximize the benefits of such learning strategies, can advance opportunities for learning in the workplace. Formal and interpersonal learning strategies that are prevalent and credible in workplace environments would be acknowledged in these models; however, informal personal learning strategies would be available as additions and alternatives for learning effective team membership. These strategies would be recognized as valid by training and development specialists as well as by the participants in this study and could be used to meet current and future workplace learning needs.

This study's findings also have implications for management personnel who are involved in or have responsibility for developing participatory practices—that is, teamwork—in the workplace. An emphasis on learning effective team membership through informal personal learning strategies could extend the manager's role to one of educator and change the work floor to an environment that fosters learning in addition to production. Knowledge of personal learning strategies and the environments that facilitate their use are invaluable to team development.

Also, team members can be empowered if the validity of informal personal learning strategies is recognized. The study participants were easily able to discuss formal strategies they used to learn to be effective team members. They were less able to discuss the informal strategies they used, however. But when they were given the opportunity to consider and articulate how they learned informally, they became aware of the power and effectiveness of informal learning strategies in facilitating their learning. The participants noted, though, that informal learning strategies carried less credibility than formal strategies in their own minds and within the organization. The lack of credibility of informal learning strategies was a disincentive to the study participants' becoming more conscious of their individual informal learning process and was a barrier to their integrating these strategies into their practice.

Finally, use of the informal personal strategies that the study participants defined as being most effective extends the level and degree of training and learning in the workplace. Changes in technology, workforce composition, economic assumptions, and international relations bring the need for new skills and thus for continuous learning. By including informal strategies in the repertoire of organizational learning opportunities, managers, supervisors, and coworkers fulfill the trainer's role and extend the community of learners. They become facilitators of learning and create a dynamic learning environment.

The benefits that have been described in this chapter can be realized by creating work floor environments that name, give credibility to, and promote informal personal learning strategies. Some of the participants in this study provided vignettes illustrating their view concerning exemplary practices and how questioning, listening, observation, reading, and reflection can be made integral parts of the work environment. These vignettes provided specific examples of a model of practice that fosters continuous learning through daily work activities. This model has three critical components: well-designed agendas for team meetings; an effective, highly interactive communication system in the workplace; and a commitment to facilitating worker inquiry. The following more fully describes the features and benefits of each of these components.

1. Well-designed agendas for team meetings
   - Foster identification and discussion of issues facing the team
   - Provide opportunities to ask questions and receive feedback about the team's direction, strategies, processes, and resources
   - Facilitate active listening by members regarding alternative perspectives or problem-solving strategies
   - Promote a variety of participatory behaviors that enable members to observe team dynamics and diverse skills and to actively engage in discussion or problem-solving activities
   - Create time and occasions for individual and group reflection on team behaviors, attitudes, goals, processes, and outcomes
   - Offer suggestions for publications that could be read, discussed, and incorporated into team members' practice
2. An effective communication system in the workplace
   - Creates and affirms spontaneous peer interactions involving information sharing, support for pressing issues, and technical assistance on interpersonal matters or skills
   - Encourages and welcomes dialogue between team leaders and members that results in a willingness to risk engaging in innovative learning projects, shared assistance in achieving individual and group goals, and support for growth and productivity
   - Facilitates individual inquiry, understanding of effective learning styles, and acquisition of needed resources
   - Provides reinforcement and affirmation of colleagues and managers as facilitators of learning.

3. A commitment to facilitating worker inquiry
    - Results in an area that contains resources—that is, materials, directories of internal and external resources and networks, and equipment that supports learning on a need-to-know basis
    - Results in coursework, seminars, and workshops that aid in skill building and complement informal learning strategies

References

Copeland, L. (1988). Learning to manage a multi-cultural workforce. *Training*, 25(5), 48–56.

Jacobs, R.C., & Everett, J. (1988). The importance of team building in a high-tech environment. *Journal of European Industrial Training*, 12(4), 10–15.

Marsick, V. J., & Watkins, K. E. (1990). *Informal and incidental learning in the workplace.* London: Routledge.

Stephans, E., Mills, G. E., Pace, R. W., & Palphs, L. (1988). Human resource development in the Fortune 500: A study. *Training and Development*, 42(1), 26–32.

How Managers Learn in the Knowledge Era

Kathleen Dechant

The Problem and the Solution. Self-directed learning ought to be natural, but questions have been raised about people's capacity to carry it out and about the support organizations can and should provide for it. By comparing self-directed learning by managers in two studies conducted approximately a decade apart, the author shows that such learning is not easy and has been made even more complex by the changing nature of managerial work. The author describes an effective way to look at planning, implementing, and evaluating self-directed learning, using an open-systems framework. She also explores challenges to self-directed learning from technology, the increasing speed of decision making in organizations, and the need to manage a decentralized workforce.

About nine years ago I studied a type of informal learning called self-directed learning (SDL), a strategy used by managers in the context of challenging job assignments (Dechant, 1989). More recently I looked at the managerial learning process as it occurs in many technology-enabled workplaces today. Although the core process of SDL remains the same, the altered organizational environment and the resulting changes in the nature of managers' jobs pose new challenges for the process. Two examples of managers from my studies illustrate this point.

Gary was a typical subject in the original study. He was a senior-level manager employed by a global manufacturing firm that was facing growing competition. He had been asked to revitalize the company's fifty-year-old core product in an attempt to improve its market share. Gary began his efforts by gathering past and present data on the product. Because he lacked knowledge of evolving government regulations relative to the product's use, he spent considerable time with the firm's legal staff. When he was certain he had internalized all he could within his own environment, he created a team of three people with complementary knowledge and skills and took them into the field. Together they lived with several of his clients over a period of several weeks, talking with them, observing them, and getting into the guts of their operations. As a result, Gary and his team discovered what few others in the company realized—that the core product really needed to be replaced, not just revitalized. The team, with Gary supervising, developed a proposal for a new product in stages, drawing in clients and organizational members as they went along. After a presentation to management, the product proposal was accepted, provoking a major change in the organization's strategy.

Jean, a participant in the later study, represents many of today's managers. Although she has an organizational background similar to Gary's, she now finds herself—as a result of reengineering and downsizing—in a smaller company and a different industry. The product is software, and the process of producing it is markedly different from the production process at her previous company. Jean's current company could be referred to as a cybercorporation, or one designed for fast change, with virtual operations and agile links between competencies (Martin, 1996). In contrast to Jean's old firm, which favored control and planning, her new firm (I'll call it "Cybercorp") is process oriented and team based, with rapid cycle times. There is more technology, a flatter structure, and fewer people. The emphasis is on innovation and time to market. Knowledge is the capital of Cybercorp. For the product development cycle to work well, knowledge must be obtained, stored, improved, and rapidly disseminated. Employees are expected to use information and communication technologies to the fullest extent possible to make this happen. The technologies most often used include a corporate intranet, voice mail, and computer conferencing.

Jean's responsibility is to manage a regional office of her company's customer response network. The network consists of hundreds of technical support people scattered throughout the country. When a customer calls in to report a problem with Cybercorp software, the call is directed to one of three centers in North America. Operators obtain a description of the problem and type all the relevant information into a database. The file is then picked up electronically by a team whose members have the skills needed to address the problem. The team is formed on-line and operates interactively over Cybercorp's intranet. No manager is involved in moving the work through the network, because the process must be seamless and fast.

Jean's job is to provide the environment needed to support the exchange of knowledge, so actions can be taken by team members to address customer problems. Because Jean's employees are so geographically dispersed, coaching is often virtual. Interactions take place more frequently through e-mail than in person. Jean travels with a laptop and routinely communicates with her regional team members by e-mail. Using the corporate intranet, she frequently inhabits a chat room where she can raise issues with her staff and receive responses within twenty-four hours.

The Studies

Both studies were qualitative interview studies. The sample for the first study consisted of twenty-one managers with ten or more years of experience who had been engaged in challenging assignments for periods of twelve to eighteen months. These managers reported two to four levels below the CEO or president. Fifteen were line managers, and six were staff. They came from the following industries: building materials, commercial banking, computer hardware and software design, management consulting, electronics, food, industrial and farm equipment, petroleum refining, pharmaceuticals, scientific and photographic equipment, and soaps and cosmetics.

The second study was conducted with sixty MBA students representing multiple industries in the New York–Connecticut–New Jersey area. They came from various functional backgrounds, including marketing, finance, sales, accounting, human resources, production operations, and engineering. Most were professionals, not managers. Their average age was twenty-nine, and they had been in their positions for from two to ten years.

Learning from Experience—The Heart of the Matter

Brockett and Hiemstra (1991) suggest a three-part definition for *self-directed learning:*

1. The individual process of planning, implementing, and evaluating learning

2. The characteristics of the learner
3. The organizational factors that facilitate or impede learning

Since on-the-job experiences form the heart of the development process for managers such as Gary and Jean, they are the primary venue for their SDL initiatives. The strategies and processes they use to learn as they work through challenging assignments, their ability to identify and address their evolving learning needs, and the nature of the environment in which they function are all key to their effectiveness on the job and to their development as managers. Even though their experiences constitute their base for learning, they must mine those experiences for that learning. Unfortunately for most managers, there exists a kind of fatalism about learning—one either does or one does not learn (Kolb, 1977).

Where to Begin? A Strategic Mindset for Learning

The second part of Brockett & Hiemstra's definition (1991) considers the characteristics of the learner. For both Gary and Jean, the ability to develop a strategic mindset for learning is a critical skill when taking on a challenging assignment. The extent to which learning will occur within such experiences depends on the degree to which managers are attentive to their environments and open to changing old mindsets when confronted with data that differs from what they have learned in the past. Because the human mind is biased in the direction of confirming rather than disconfirming information, the more successful learners are those who are vigilant and actively seek out data that calls for them to alter previously held ideas and practices, even when those ideas and practices have proven successful in the past (R. Velk, personal communication, 1989). Therefore, if Gary and Jean are to be effective at SDL, they must possess a strategic mindset for learning and expect all their experiences to be sources of learning and change.

Linking Strategy to Process: A Systems Approach to SDL

An effective way to look at the process of planning, implementing, and evaluating learning is to use an open-systems framework. The use of such a framework for approaching on-the-job learning is based on the assumption that the system—that is, the manager in situ—is constantly interacting with the environment. Systems theory is an appropriate way to illustrate the interdependency between a learner and his or her environment because it assumes that learning is holistic rather than analytic (Schoderbek, Schoderbek, & Kefalas, 1990). The risk of not taking a holistic approach to viewing learning is the tendency to focus on a particular aspect of managerial learning, such as learning style, without regard for the context in which the learning is embedded. The nature of the organization, the constraints of the environment, the presence of others as sources of and collaborators in learning—all go unnoticed and unaccounted for. When an individual is considered to be an open system, it is relatively easy to see how the environment affects and is affected by that person as a learner (Dechant, 1996). A manager in a state of conscious attentiveness, as described earlier, is able to more rapidly assimilate the learning that experiences offer and to take appropriate action.

The SDL process using the systems model described previously is one in which a manager begins with three types of inputs: the specific goals of an assignment, the skills required by the task, and an initial strategy for learning (whether conscious or not). As mentioned earlier, managers who are very effective at SDL have an intentional strategy more often than not. They define the issues to be investigated in light of the task goals, selecting the means to investigate the relevant issues and identifying both informal and formal methods to close knowledge and skill gaps. Some questions to ask at this point are the following:

1. Is there any situational history? Who knows it?
2. To what extent is the vision for the task or assignment clear to the manager? The organization?
3. What are the information and learning needs of parties critical to the completion of the task or assignment?
4. What specific outputs does the manager expect? The organization? Other interested parties?

The sense-making process that occurs next, as a manager interacts with the situation, is most often a matter of informal inquiry, which involves other individuals as sources of information and interpretation (Louis, 1985). The manager evolves an idiosyncratic or highly textured meaning scheme for the rapidly unfolding situation, in collaboration with others (Brown, 1989). Managers who are attentive to the nuances of situations as they encounter them alter their behavior in response to such contextual clues. They modify their focus, priorities, and behavior—even

▲ Figure 5.1 A Systems View of Self-Directed Learning

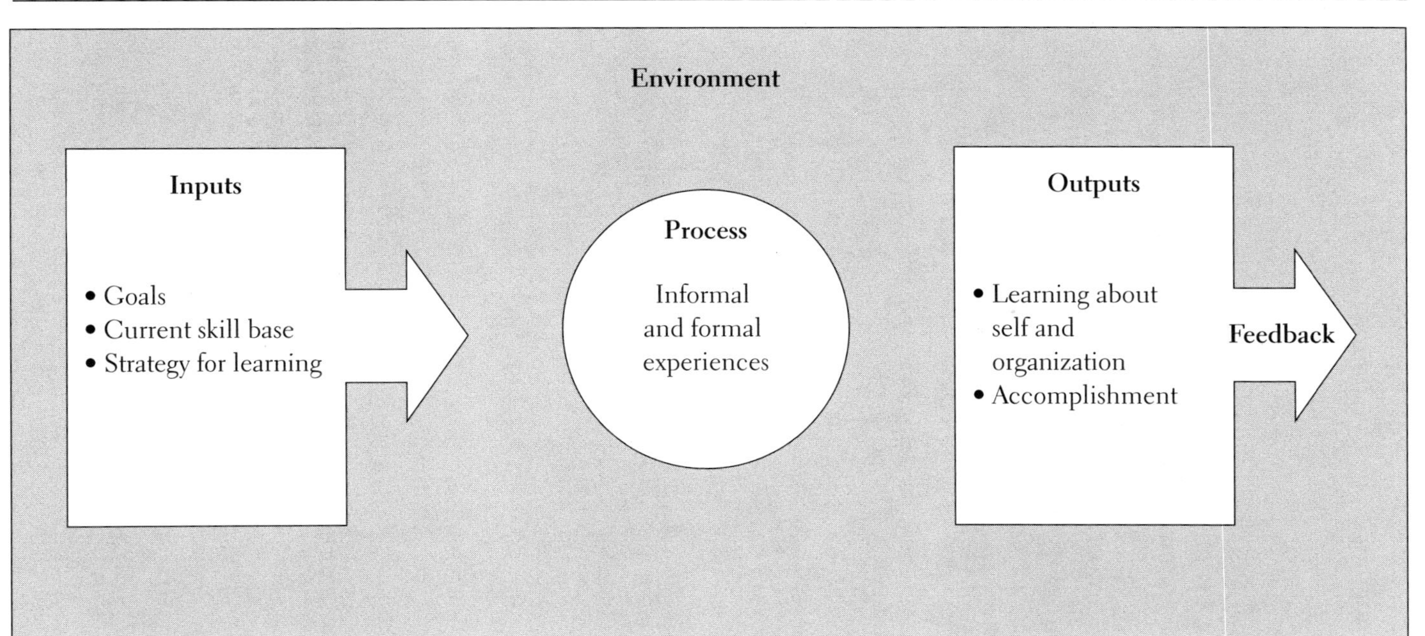

their managerial style—according to feedback from the environment. These modifications are the outcomes of situational learning. Those managers who are not open to situations as opportunities for learning or who are unable to hear the feedback from situations that call for change tend to rely on old mindsets and behavioral repertoires. They are unable or unwilling to examine and challenge assumptions grounded in past experiences. As a result, they do not learn and end up taking actions that are inappropriate or ineffective (Weick, 1983; Langer, 1989).

The process can also include inquiry in a more formal context. For example, a manager can participate in a training program, conference, or some structured learning activity specifically designed by others to give the manager the requisite knowledge.

The output of the learning process includes the completed task as well as what is learned about oneself and the organization. A critical aspect of the output is feedback that helps to evaluate the effectiveness of action taken and becomes part of the input into the next round of SDL. As such, feedback enables the manager to identify new learning needs even as old ones are resolved. The effectiveness of managers at learning and performing increases as they construct and use multiple sources of feedback, particularly when circumstances are ambiguous. Feedback becomes a beacon that illuminates and guides action in addition to revealing emerging learning needs.

Lessons Learned

An examination of the contrast between the environments of Jean's and Gary's organizations provides insights into the different challenges for these two managers as self-directed learners. Because Gary is in a traditional bureaucratic and hierarchical organization, part of his effectiveness is his ability to work the system vertically and laterally. His interactions with people occur in real time and are primarily face to face. Of course, technologies such as the phone, voice mail, and faxes are also involved. However, it is obvious that Gary's collaboration with his team and his customers is a personal and direct one. He relies on the observed reactions of others for instant feedback on actions planned or taken.

Gary's need for structured learning experiences is limited to a few formal sessions with consultants and some briefings by government postal authorities. Again, these occur in real time and are face-to-face interactions. In terms of overall skill development, Gary's education as a manager was linked to his ascent through the ranks; he was sent to both in-house and external training programs as he advanced.

Jean's challenges with SDL were in three areas: dependence on technology to expedite information and create knowledge, accelerated expectations concerning knowledge exchange and interpretation, and management of a virtual workforce. In her previous situation, Jean, like Gary, was accustomed to operating in a clearly defined hierarchy where information moved up and down established channels. It was fairly obvious in that organization where one needed to go to get answers. Because data was generally confined to the same geographical boundaries occupied by both management and staff, self-directed learning activities mostly involved making a phone call or visit to a peer, manager, or subordinate. In Cybercorp, however, the answers to questions are complex and are scattered in dozens of databases over several network connections. The only way to find information is to use the technological infrastructure to access it. Furthermore, because data is available in great amounts and turnaround is expected quickly, Jean had to develop better analytic skills. Locating, linking, and making sense of the bits of data floating around Cybercorp's memory banks requires a higher level of conceptualization. For example, Jean must be able to comprehend emerging patterns of customer needs within her region based on various reports, team problem-solving activities, and marketplace data, all of which are located in disparate databanks. Finally, because learning is happening simultaneously for dozens of her people at the same time in different locations, information is in constant flux. Jean needs to serve as a central collection and interpretation point. She is at the heart of a network of knowledge workers. Jean must help other knowledge workers make sense of what she knows, and she must interpret, analyze, and synthesize what they know.

Looking Forward

In the course of carrying out challenging assignments, managers may or may not learn. As Jarvis (1987) observed, "learning and experience are not synonymous; an individual may grow and develop as a result of a learning experience or may remain virtually unaltered" (pp. 17, 24). For managers in contemporary organizations to become effective at SDL, they must strive to learn in a thinking manner. Borrowing from Weick's theory (1983) of managerial thought, managers learn in a thinking manner when they demonstrate "various amounts of deliberateness, intention, care, control and pertinence" in their learning processes (p. 223). This is true of all managers, but it is particularly true in companies that rely heavily on information technology for communication and for information creation and dissemination.

From these two representative cases it is clear that the differences in organizational environments brought on by technological infrastructures have altered the process of SDL. As a result, Cybercorpian managers must develop new and improved skills related to learning from experience. The nature and pace of learning at Cybercorp and similar firms suggest that their managers must have a higher capacity for self-direction than do managers in more traditional organizations. In such organizations, a manager who is effective at SDL is one who

- Is perpetually learning
- Is comfortable with technology
- Is open to frequent change
- Provides more and more frequent feedback
- Is a rapid sense maker and sense giver

Those with low capacity in these areas will become frustrated and disenchanted, despite the many opportunities for learning and growth afforded by environments in which technology is a mainstay of management.

References

Brockett, R. G., & Hiemestra, R. (1991). *Self-direction in adult learning: Perspectives on theory, research, and practice.* London: Routledge & Kegan Paul.

Brown, J. S. (April, 1989). *Toward a new epistemology for learning.* Paper based on an address at the American Educational Research Association meeting, San Francisco.

Dechant, K. (1989). *Managing change in the workplace: Learning strategies of managers.* Unpublished doctoral dissertation, Teachers College, Columbia University.

Dechant, K. (1996). The playing fields of learning. In S. Cavaleri & D. Fearon (Eds.), *Managing in organizations that learn* (pp. 97–118). Cambridge, MA: Blackwell.

Jarvis, P. (1987). *Adult learning in the social context.* London: Croom-Helm.

Kolb, D. (1977). On management and the learning process. In D. A. Kolb (Ed.), *Organizational psychology: A book of readings* (2nd ed.). Englewood Cliffs, NJ: Prentice Hall.

Langer, E. (1989). *Mindfulness.* Reading, MA: Addison-Wesley.

Louis, M. R. (1985). Introduction: Perspectives on organizational culture. In P. J. Frost, L. F. Moore, M. R. Louis, C. C. Lundburg, & J. Martin (Eds.), *Organizational culture* (pp. 27–30). Beverly Hills, CA: Sage.

Martin, J. (1996). *Cybercorp: The new business revolution.* New York: AMACOM.

Schoderbek, P. P., Schoderbek, C. G., & Kefalas, A. G. (1990). *Management systems: Conceptual considerations.* Boston: Irwin.

Weick, K. (1983). Managerial thought in the context of action. In S. Shrivastva & Associates (Eds.), *The executive mind* (pp. 221–242). San Francisco: Jossey-Bass.

"Awakening": Developing Learning Capacity in a Small Family Business

Mary Ziegler

The Problem and the Solution. Small family businesses face unique challenges due to their size and the fact that decisions made by family members are often not open to discussion or challenge. Yet such businesses face pressures to transform the way their managers and employees work and learn, just as larger businesses do. This chapter discusses informal learning strategies observed in a family publishing company undergoing a business transformation. The author describes "awakening," the first phase of the change process, and the implications for practice it presents.

The concept of a learning organization holds tremendous promise for small businesses as they stretch to meet the demands of a changing business environment, yet there are few documented examples of small family businesses that commit to this effort. This chapter tells the story of "Hardesty Enterprises" (a fictitious name for the company examined in this study) and how its owners and managers learned what it takes to transform a small company into a learning organization. Because many small businesses face similar challenges to their survival and growth, the story of Hardesty Enterprises can help owners of other small businesses as they make decisions about managing change.

The Study

The study contrasted the real-world context of a small family business with the components of a learning organization described in the literature. A learning organization is one that continually expands its capacity to create desired results; uses learning as an intentional, strategic tool for organizational and individual advancement; and facilitates learning for all its members by removing barriers (Pedler, Burgoyne, & Boydell, 1991; Senge, 1990; Watkins & Marsick, 1993).

The story of Hardesty Enterprises' change process is based on an interpretive case study using qualitative data. The research set out to assess how the owners and managers of Hardesty Enterprises perceived the changes that occurred in the company approximately eight months after they began their effort to intentionally become a learning organization. The study population consisted of the company's owners and managers, because they were actively involved during the first stage of the change initiative. Data were collected from a wide variety of sources, including interviews and company documents. The study addressed several questions:

- How does learning become part of the fabric of a business culture?
- How does a company develop the capacity to become a learning organization?
- Is organizational learning different from individual learning, and if so, how is it different?

"Awakening" at Hardesty Enterprises

Hardesty Enterprises is a holding company consisting of two operating companies: Hardesty Printing and Community Poster. Although the two companies operated separately at the time of the study, their futures were intertwined, as the company was embarking on a journey toward fundamental change. Hardesty Printing was founded in 1944 when John Hardesty began a small family-owned commercial printing company in the Southeast. Hardesty's two sons were exposed to the business, and by the age of sixteen had worked in most of the company's departments. Like many other children of parents who owned small businesses, the Hardesty sons went to work in their father's company directly after high school. Eventually Ted (the older son) succeeded his father as president of the company, and Tom (the younger son) became director of sales. The company eventually grew to 150 employees, with sales of more than

$12 million. John Hardesty began his second company in 1968 when he took a picture of his daughter Ann's marching band and printed it on a poster. He raised donations for the band by selling advertising on the poster. Ann took a leadership role in the new company after only a year of college.

Hardesty Printing and Community Poster grew and thrived for more than forty-five years. By the early 1990s both companies were experiencing increasing business volume but decreasing profits. Dwindling confidence in a secure future for the company troubled the owners and executive managers. Increases in federal regulations taxed their system to its limit. Dramatic changes in printing technology required major capital investments in new equipment and new technical expertise. Over the years, Hardesty Printing and Community Poster had tried to be innovative and had tried to explore ways to bring the companies back to life, but most of those efforts had failed or had only highlighted the growing extent of their problems.

The company awoke to the fact that it could not continue on its present well-worn path and expect to survive the decade. The owners began looking for guidance. At that point they discovered the idea of the learning organization. They hired consultants to help them learn how to understand and implement the concept. The intentional change effort began in July 1993, when consultants helped the three owners clarify their vision for the company. Although the process focused on an assortment of factors, the most prominent factor was learning. One of the owners, talking about implementing an intentional learning process, said, "This is going to be the toughest thing we ever did . . . to change the way people think and act."

Hardesty Enterprises had operated for more than forty years as a hierarchical organization. Its structure was pyramidal, with knowledge and authority residing at the top. The owners envisioned a flattened organizational structure that would distribute knowledge, responsibility, and authority throughout the organization. The Hardesty family had no way of knowing about the daily operations of a learning organization, because there were few documented examples. True pioneers, they learned their way into fundamentally changing their companies. Ironically, those who had learned the most probably would not identify the changes they made as being the result of learning. Two formal training events were used to launch the change initiative. These events set off a chain reaction of informal learning processes that lasted long after the training was over.

The first phase of the learning process at Hardesty Enterprises can be characterized as an "awakening." The study participants described this "awakening" metaphorically, as "opening the door," "throwing out old trash," "a new beginning," "removing shrouds of darkness," "realizing how big the world really is," "opening my eyes," and "recovering from being a zombie." The metaphors speak to the potential for renewal. The respondents gave the impression that Hardesty Enterprises, especially Hardesty Printing, was metaphorically like an old factory with dim lights, closed windows, and piles of old trash. The very idea of change, even if it was not fully understood, acted like a mental spring cleaning. Lights were turned on to current practices, windows were opened to new ideas, and old trash was sold or thrown away to make space (sometimes literally). The very idea of learning stimulated actual learning.

Awakening included imagining, using metaphors, what it would be like to learn to change the forty-five-year-old company. A manager described the process this way: "I keep looking at it as this avalanche thing. There is this ten-thousand-pound boulder, and you have to move it one mile. Fortunately, you only have to push it one inch, because the rest of the mile is off a cliff and gravity will take care of it. But it is moving that ten-thousand-pound boulder that is where we are now. If we can just get past this, we will be unstoppable."

Informal Learning Processes

Informal learning was central to the way the company's owners, managers, and employees made sense of what it meant to make themselves and their company into a new image. Those involved in the change made sense of what they were experiencing by means of three learning processes: making meaning, challenging mental models, and learning how to do new things.

Making Meaning

The first step in learning was for the company's managers and employees to interpret the new situation in which they found themselves. They made meaning by making connections. Meaning grew slowly, like a crystal forming, as people perceived how new developments were in some way like familiar experiences. In making these connections, the study participants could see how each new change was really a lot like other events from the company's past.

People learned about connections by asking questions that enabled them to dig more deeply into the thinking behind a new way of doing things. One owner commented, "Understanding the 'whys' has a lot more to do with things than understanding the 'hows' and the techniques and the daily activities." Understanding the "whys" is at the heart of learning. Or, put another way, "'why' is really the theory that is behind the procedure." Understanding the reasons for things is what got lost over the years as the companies grew. Asking "why" changed over time from being a way to threaten people to being a way to understand people.

People created shared meaning as they inquired into what terms and events meant and then defined those terms and events themselves to clarify their experience. They created shared meanings from common interpretations of events. For example, when members of the communication team took the time to describe what communication looked and felt like, they began to operate from a common, collective reference point. Dialogue and discussion in committees or teams led people to reframe their original thoughts, based on new information. Before teams were formed, knowledge resided mainly in the heads of individuals. There was very little reason to share that knowledge or acquire new learning so that it could be shared with others. Working in teams across boundaries, people began to develop new, collective understandings of the organizational world they were shaping.

Challenging Mental Models

A second learning process in which people in these companies engaged was to challenge their mental models, which Senge (1990) describes as people's taken-for-granted assumptions about reality. Mental models are so deeply ingrained that people are not normally aware of their existence. Mental models can be individual, or they can be shared by groups of people. Organizations that want to transform have to examine and reassess these mental models; nothing can be taken for granted.

The owners and managers at Hardesty Enterprises uncovered and challenged mental models in three ways: by attending to and reflecting on what was normally considered familiar, by becoming more aware of assumptions, and by actively challenging beliefs. Through the first process people attended to their actions and thoughts or environment by consciously noticing these things and becoming more aware of them. Many behaviors and thoughts become automatic or habitual. They are so familiar that they are no longer considered worthy of one's attention. A manager from Community Poster described this habitual action this way: "For example, every day you walk by this picture of a tree. Then something happens, and one day you look at the picture of the tree differently. And you see a flower at the bottom of the tree, and you say, 'Oh, look at that pretty flower!' You looked at that picture every day. But you never noticed the flower before." The study participants described seeing things that they knew had always been there but had never seen before.

Assumptions often guide behavior. By making assumptions explicit that are normally implicit, people can be made uncomfortable, but they have to ask whether they are doing things in the best way. As one manager put it, "Our lack of structure in the organization makes a person have to guess what's the right thing to do." Many people suggested that the organization engaged people in relatively mindless "activity-preventing thinking." An executive maintained, "Used to [be] we didn't think of stuff. We were all going about our business trying to do things." As people began to uncover assumptions and develop a new awareness, they began to challenge and change their beliefs.

Challenging beliefs is at the heart of change. "Struggle" was frequently used to describe how people changed their thinking. An enlightened supervisor said, "It takes a while to change your thinking. But you have to change how you think before you can change the way you do things." Those involved in the change effort at Hardesty Enterprises began to shift their thinking by viewing their environment in new ways. However, they also noticed that new thinking loses its value if it is not followed by a change in how things are done.

Learning How to Do Things Differently

The study participants reported that they acquired new and wide-ranging skills that fell primarily into three main categories: general interpersonal skills, cognitive skills, and technical skills. Most individuals described the nature of management and supervision as being primarily interpersonal, even though learning how to manage in the new environment also involved having some technical skills. When talking about becoming a more effective manager, for example, one respondent said, "I learned a little bit about listening. I say a little bit because it is really hard to do and I struggle with it." Many people became aware of the major role played by the relationships individuals had with one another and of how difficult it was to communicate effectively within many of those relationships. It may be that these relationships were even more complex because people had developed long, strong family or friendship ties.

People at Hardesty Enterprises had always paid attention to acquiring cognitive skills, but this kind of learning was never as intentional or purposive as it became after the change initiative began. Cognitive skills were cultivated as people began to document existing work processes, identify problems, search for root causes, and formulate solutions.

The people at the company also developed new technical skills. People learned these skills primarily within the context of everyday work. They learned team meeting skills in actual team meetings. They developed problem-solving skills as they followed actual processes in the plant. They learned computer skills creating project management charts or completing a job for a customer using a new computer tool. Learning was not separate from work; work provided a context so that the learning made sense.

Translating Insight and New Thinking into Behavior

The learning process at Hardesty Enterprises was elusive. In analyzing it, the exact point at which learning took place was very difficult to locate. Learning occurred when experience was transformed into new knowledge, skills, or attitudes that led to changed behavior. Not surprisingly, the most difficult part of the process for many of the study participants was translating new insights and thinking into new behavior. It was relatively easy to master new theories about the learning organization, the quality movement, leadership, and personal mastery. Owners and managers were able to create a new organizational model that helped them make sense of experiences that otherwise might have seemed senseless or uncomfortable. But it was extremely difficult to change behaviors that were deeply ingrained. An owner described this challenge:

> Well, I guess the challenge is your own previous design of yourself. You know, trying to change that. Let's say your belief has been changed, really

> changed. . . . I guess the challenge is applying the theories, applying your changed beliefs, on a daily basis. You get so consumed in learning that it occupies so much that you can't even think about application. . . . When somebody asks you a question, you want to go through your top ten theories and principles and react from one of those. But you don't. You just react. And your reaction is diametrically opposed to the new theories and things you really believe.

The images used by this participant reveal the complexity of translating theory (changed beliefs) into practice (new behavior that a person really wants but is unable to adopt). As he explained, the machine (a person's mind) still has the same parts in it, and it wants to keep responding the way it has responded in the past. And even though beliefs have changed, responses triggered by habit fly in the face of the new beliefs. As one participant said, "You have to throw the switch," describing the process of changing automatic behavior into behavior one is aware of.

Familiar triggers evoke familiar responses. Changed beliefs cause the process to be less automatic and more reflective. Although the reaction to the trigger is the same, what has changed is the awareness of the disjuncture between changed beliefs and automatic behavior. An executive explained it this way: "We know what we are supposed to do. We are supposed to listen and understand and restate what the person said in order to clarify. We aren't supposed to judge. We know these things. But how you actually get it to happen is much more difficult than it sounds, because people get emotional about their beliefs." This individual went on to explain that in the heat of a discussion, it is very difficult to practice good communication techniques one has learned.

In the change process, the old and the new exist side by side. An executive said that it was almost as if the company were maintaining "a dual system. . . . People will be listening to you and you will feel pretty good about it. Then you will turn around and run into a thirty-year-old situation where you feel totally like a pawn in some game. You will experience both those things. In fact, they could happen within thirty minutes of each other."

The saying "easier said than done" captures the feelings of people as they tried to put the concepts presented by the consultants into practice. One manager said he was able to tell the employees in his department what the new concepts were and how the company wanted employees to be involved. But he said he could not tell them how this would change anything they were doing in their department. The theories were clearer than their application to the everyday life of the company.

Awakening: The First Stage of the Learning Process

Most executives were aware of the gap between theory and practice. This gap was best characterized as a continuum that individuals and organizations move along as they change. "Awakening" describes the first step of the change process. Insight is that first step—the "awakening" that starts the learning process. One of the owners described it this way: "It's almost like you [had] operated like a zombie before. Whatever it was that you were doing for the last fifteen years, you finally ask, 'Why do I do that?' You almost forgot you had theories [assumptions] behind what you were doing and why you were doing it. And [behind] what you thought. Instead you just did it."

The metaphor of the zombie indicates the way many of the study participants viewed Hardesty Enterprises before it embarked on becoming a learning organization—as a company that had died but continued to move about. A lifeless company, in their view, is one that behaves without mindfulness. The desire to change their company caused them to be mindful of their current situation in a way they had not done before. Change through learning held the promise of bringing life back to the company.

Most of the study participants spoke of learning in terms of learning *how* to do something. Few thought of learning in terms of making meaning, challenging mental models, experimenting, or learning *why* to do something. Yet it was clear to me that the owners and managers were indeed engaging in the latter activities and were thereby moving in the direction of becoming a learning organization. The study participants probably would not say that they consciously and intentionally learned by reflecting on their present circumstances. Their reflection occurred more as a byproduct of their trying to identify current practices in departments or of their creating flowcharts of work processes. Some people compared what was described in books they had read with the reality they observed in the plant. Their learning was a reflective process but not necessarily a *consciously* reflective one. Reflection occurred as Dewey (1938) describes it occurring: as a state of doubt or perplexity followed by searching for a resolution. For some, the state of doubt arose as they examined long-standing practices and began to question their effectiveness. It was this process that uncovered people's assumptions and beliefs.

Moving from Individual Learning to Collective Learning

The experiential learning processes described in the literature (Kolb, 1984; Jarvis, 1987) are much more linear than the learning processes I observed at Hardesty Enterprises. The way learning happened there is not unlike the way the president of the company described his decision-making style: "plan, aim, plan some more, aim, take a little shot, study, plan some more, aim, and then finally shoot." Learning was an iterative, experimental process that involved both individual learning and group (including dyad) learning. Individuals shared ideas, experiences, or insights with one another, reflected on the sharing activity, and then shared again.

The act of sharing had two consequences. First, sharing often changed the meaning of the information, experience, or insight that was shared. Second, once shared, the information, experience, or insight had the potential to become collective meaning (that is, it had the potential to be understood in the same way by the individuals sharing it). This may (or may not) have then led to organizational learning. At Hardesty Enterprises there was a dynamic link between individual learning and collective learning. Individuals created meaning from their experiences in discussions among one another. Sharing became the mechanism that linked individual learning with organizational learning.

The distinctive feature of collective learning at Hardesty Enterprises, as is so in other studies, was the sharing of insights, knowledge, assumptions, understandings, interpretations, patterns of thought, and mental maps (Argyris & Schön, 1978; Jelenick, 1979; Senge & Sterman, 1992; Shrivastava, 1983; Stata, 1989). The only way that people could generate a shared vision was through collective meaning making. When individuals shared their ideas about the change the company was undergoing and compared their ideas with those of others, they created collective meaning. When individuals participated on a committee or team and struggled to define terms and collectively inquire into current practices, they created collective meaning.

The literature on organizational learning does not capture the richness of the actual experience. "Awakening" implies a collective heuristic that takes place when a group goes through a process of discovery. This research supports the notion that organizations can be sensitized to learning. But the description of how that occurs typically does not speak to the complexity of being awakened by new information and the subsequent process by which people use new information to test and change their assumptions. It also does not adequately describe the difficulty people have in translating a changed assumption into a new action.

This gap between theory and action—the inability to convert new convictions into practice—is a critical juncture in the learning process. It is often at this point that learning is truncated, because the individual or group cannot accomplish what they believe they want: "It's easier said than done." The gap presents a challenge for the adult educator or human resources professional, whose role then becomes to help the learning individual or group to bridge this gap.

It would be difficult to claim that by the time this study concluded, Hardesty Enterprises had become a learning organization. But as Gertrude Stein said, "There is no there, there." A learning organization is not a destination but a way of working and being together as an organization. The changes taking place at Hardesty Enterprises began to develop its capacity to learn at all levels.

Lessons Learned

How does learning become part of the fabric of a family business's culture? Hardesty Enterprises has shown us that, in the beginning stages at least, commitment by owners to their own learning makes a strong impression on employees. Examining one's business practices has the potential to expose "old skeletons in the closet," as one participant said, and therefore takes courage as well as commitment. And finally—and perhaps most important—the owners chose a path for the company that almost no one understood. By choosing this path of discovery, they ensured that learning would be the only alternative, for themselves and for the company as a whole. The learning process is far more ambiguous, messy, and elusive in reality than what is depicted in the popular management literature.

To recap, five key lessons learned at Hardesty Enterprises are as follows. First, informal learning processes characterize the beginning stage of an intentional organizational change. Learning begins by making meaning, which includes achieving clarity of purpose, inquiring, defining terms, and sharing meaning. People are then led to challenge mental models and to learn how to do new things.

Second, the gap that exists between having insights and changing behavior can severely constrain learning outcomes and cause a good deal of pain and frustration. It is possible to be exposed to new ideas, to enthusiastically adopt new ideas, and still to be unable to apply those ideas. At Hardesty Enterprises, those who had adopted new beliefs often found it difficult to put them into practice, and they became very frustrated with themselves and with the learning process. Excessive frustration can be an obstacle to learning.

Third, the old and the new often coexist side by side. Learning outcomes are situational. Organizations do not change overnight from being one way to being another way. Change is developmental and occurs along a continuum. New thinking does not replace old thinking, so that the old thinking no longer exists. In one situation it may be very possible to think and act according to a new belief, whereas in another situation the new belief may not emerge at all. In the midst of a learning process, inconsistency is likely.

Fourth, for a small family business to change to a learning organization, the owners and other family members must be committed to their own learning. As many members of the organization as possible must also be involved in learning. Creating a learning organization in a family firm in which the family actively participates would be very difficult without the willingness of the family members to engage in their own learning and self-examination. Their commitment to learning must be visible to others in the organization.

Finally, a learning organization is intensely colored by the culture from which it grows. Hardesty Enterprises developed its own model of a learning organization. The way learning is expressed at Hardesty Enterprises will be uniquely the company's own. The same will most likely be true for other organizations.

Eight months after the change initiative began, there was evidence that certain activities and conditions had helped Hardesty Enterprises on its journey to becoming a learning organization. The company awakened to the need to learn a new way of being in the world. This "awakening" was an important step. Because of it, the owners began to acknowledge their problems, look for solutions, and open themselves to new ideas.

"Awakening" may look different for different organizations; the following factors were important at Hardesty Enterprises:

- The owners made a public commitment to their own learning. by word and example.
- The owners were willing to be open about what they did not know.
- Management (and others) understood the reasons why change was needed.
- People increased their awareness of the company as a total system by documenting and analyzing the areas where departments and functions were interconnected.
- Individual managers experimented with changing relationships by identifying current management practices and the assumptions that underlie them.
- As many people as possible were involved in learning activities, both individually and collectively.
- Results of learning and descriptions of learning were broadly shared throughout the organization.
- Teams had opportunities to learn while they were solving company problems.
- Learning activities took place in the context of real work that was meaningful.
- People identified small learning projects that had a strong possibility for success.
- Skill training helped people develop tools that encouraged learning at different levels.

Finally, the study found that Hardesty Enterprises made progress toward its goal of becoming an organization that learns. Individual learning was documented, as was group learning. The owners knew that they did not want to continue operating the way they had operated in the past, yet they had no map to guide them to a different future. At the outset, the need for individual and collective learning was the only thing about which they were absolutely sure.

The idea of "becoming a learning organization" suggests that it is a destination to be reached or a specific goal to be achieved. But transformative learning assumes that such a destination or goal will always by necessity be changing and thus remain beyond reach. "Are we there yet?" one might ask. In the learning model of organizations, one can never answer that question. Rather than a destination, a learning organization is a state of being. Certainty must be suspended for the sake of discovery—an often simultaneously frightening and exhilarating experience. In an organization that learns, the best answer is no longer owned by experts or executive managers.

For the owners of Hardesty Enterprises, the learning organization may be more a yearning than a reality—an ideal to fuel their energy for the challenge of learning and necessary change. The Hardesty family truly are pioneers who are forging a way for others to follow. With great courage they are learning to create a better future for themselves and their employees—one based on full participation for all members. For them and for many other individuals and organizations, the elusive idea of the learning organization holds great promise.

References

Argyris, C., & Schön, D. (1978). *Organizational learning: A theory of action perspective.* Reading, MA: Addison-Wesley.

Dewey, J. (1938). *Experience and education.* New York: Macmillan.

Jarvis, P. (1987). *Adult learning in the social context.* London: Croom-Helm.

Jelenick, M. (1979). *Institutionalizing innovation: A study of organizational learning systems.* New York: Praeger.

Kolb (1984). *Experiential learning.* Englewood Cliffs, NJ: Prentice-Hall.

Pedler, M., Burgoyne, J., & Boydel, T. (1991). *The learning company: A strategy for sustainable development.* New York: McGraw-Hill.

Senge, P. M. (1990). *The fifth discipline: The art and practice of the learning organization.* New York: Doubleday.

Senge, P. M., & Sterman, J. D. (1992). Systems thinking and organizational learning: Acting locally and thinking globally in the organizations of the future. *European Journal of Operational Research,* 59, 137–150.

Shrivastava, P. (1983). A typology of organizational learning systems. *Journal of Management Studies,* 20(1), 7–28.

Stata, R. (1989, Spring). Organizational learning—The key to management innovation. *Sloan Management Review,* pp. 63–74.

Watkins, K. E., & Marsick, V. J. (1993). *Sculpting the learning organization: Lessons in the art and science of systemic change.* San Francisco: Jossey-Bass.

Critical Reflection as a Response to Organizational Disruption

Ann K. Brooks

The Problem and the Solution. Organizations going through radical change seem to invite questioning of their fundamental assumptions, values, and beliefs as a step toward achieving deep change. Yet little is known about whether or not such questioning actually takes place, how it can be facilitated, and what conditions are needed to support it. This study, in a Baby Bell company that was undergoing divestiture, found that some employees did think critically and that this sometimes led to dilemmas, "punishments," and challenges to the organization's leadership. Strategies that helped employees develop critically reflective thinking included exposure to different perspectives, liberal arts courses, open-ended assignments, modeling, encouragement of questioning, honest feedback, and participation in policymaking and policy implementation.

In this chapter I revisit an earlier study I conducted on critical and reflective learning among managers in organizations undergoing transformative change, using the lens of informal learning. Although the data I collected for that study clearly indicated that the phenomenon of informal learning was present, I did not originally analyze it for this purpose.

The organization I studied was one of the "Baby Bell" telephone companies. I began the study shortly after the company's usual way of doing business was radically disrupted by its legally mandated divestiture from AT&T in 1984. All of the Baby Bell companies embarked on a journey of change intended to transform them from tightly regulated, policy-driven bureaucracies into what was hoped would be lean, competitive, entrepreneurial corporations capable of competing in the open marketplace (Tunstall, 1986).

In stable organizations, learning usually focuses on the transfer of skills and knowledge and the socialization of employees. The employees at the subject company were being asked to reconceptualize their work, their way of relating to one another, and the way they set their goals (Sonnenfeld, 1985; Brooks, 1992). The game they had learned to play as employees was changing—they were not clear what constituted a home run anymore, and the bases would not stay still.

At the time I conducted the study, "critical reflection" was the only learning construct I could find that addressed the learning these employees seemed to require (Freire, 1972; Mezirow, 1981; Brookfield, 1987). Critical reflection in organizations is rarely a formal activity. Fundamental to informal critically reflective learning is the ability to ask questions. Making inquiries stands as the only method we have to break us out of the worldviews we take for granted. The phenomenon of critical questioning, then—including how it is developed, how it is used, and the degree of support it receives from other employees—emerges as the central issue for understanding informal critically reflective learning in organizations.

Up until the 1970s, learning continued to be viewed synonymously with training (education for lower-level employees), development (education mostly for midlevel and upper-level managers), and "forums" (education for executives). Most corporations continued to spend enormous sums of money to provide an array of training and development opportunities for their employees, with little consideration for the companies' needs or the ability of training to address problems that had been identified.

The concept of organizational learning that began to emerge in the mid–1980s had the potential to invigorate the role in the creation of learning systems (Fiol & Lyles, 1985). The central question in organizational theory was finally shifting away from what organizations' form should be (an essentialist approach in which a universal, "right" form for organizations was sought) to how organizations can become ongoing systems of learning. To begin to address this challenge, human resources professionals and other functional managers and executives had to break with their assumptions about their organizations and their work and begin to reflect critically on what they had taken for granted. Most importantly, they had to challenge their own assumptions about education, training, and development and the place of these heretofore formal functions in organizations.

The study's principal assumption was that employees in organizations undergoing radical change who experienced a radical disruption of what they had assumed to be correct and true needed to be able to reflect critically on themselves and their organization. Although the questions I initially posed in the study did not address informal learning, much of what the participants had to say turned out to be important to understanding the concept.

The Study

The study was designed as a single qualitative case study. I sought research participants who could be characterized as having demonstrated an ability to reflect critically on themselves, their company, or both. Because the concept of critical reflection had been developed within the context of theory or practice rather than research (Freire, 1972; Mezirow, 1981; Brookfield, 1987), it had not been developed operationally, and no instrument existed to identify individuals capable of critical reflection. This precluded any attempts to "measure" critical thinking in the conventional way at the time. What was additionally confounding was that scholars did not agree on terminology.

It was within this context that I asked the corporation's senior internal organizational development consultant to identify as many people as he could whom he thought questioned the status quo and regularly took action to make change happen. I then contacted the people he identified and asked them the same question. Of the individuals those people named, I selected the twenty-one managers who received the most nominations. The final group of twenty-nine study participants included those twenty-one (who ranged from entry-level managers up to and including the chairman and CEO), four who had been consistently named as *not* being critically reflective, and four who had been consistently named as having made a dramatic shift from not being critically reflective to being so. Two images were used by many individuals to describe the critically reflective participants. The first was that they "can see the emperor is wearing no clothes"; the second was that they "are troublemakers." Being called a troublemaker did not appear to be regarded as bad—several people used the term to describe the chairman and CEO, a man who seemed to be generally admired and respected for his leadership and integrity.

The phenomenon of critical questioning—including how it was developed, how it is used, and the degree of support it receives from other employees—emerges as the central issue for understanding informal critically reflective learning in organizations. In fact, very little reformulation of the original data is required to see the functions of critically reflective learning, how upper-level management encouraged or discouraged it, and how critically reflective learning skills were developed among employees.

Findings

Fostering informal learning in organizations requires an understanding of how such learning functions, how it is either encouraged or discouraged by managers, and how the organizational environment can facilitate or impede it. The following paragraphs look at each of these aspects.

Functions of Critically Reflective Learning

Critical reflection is useful for improving work practices, addressing moral and ethical dilemmas, and evaluating organizational goals and strategies. A practical means of assessing the value of critical reflection is to measure whether it improves work practices. For example, critical reflection was used informally at the subject company to improve work practices in the area of employee career development. The change concerned hiring and promotion practices for management-level employees. Traditionally career moves were decided solely by managers or supervisors. They decided where the employees under them went. As one manager noted, the whole process of how these decisions were made shifted to employees, "and that was a real change . . . because . . . the employee didn't generally even see the requisition unless the supervisor came and showed it to him. Your career decisions were not yours to make. The company told you. Very, very, patriarchal. . . . [The] whole thing [that is, the change] came out of the reflections of [our group, which said] 'What are our real values here? What do we believe? What's wrong with this picture?'" The group's critical reflection produced a change so powerful that the entire company ultimately adopted it. In terms of learning systems, the learning occurred within the context of a work or functional group and then spread to the entire organization.

Critical reflection can lead to the uncovering of moral and ethical dilemmas that need to be resolved. However, informal critical reflection is not always met with a welcoming embrace. It can be rejected, leaving an employee isolated. For example, one employee stated that when she critically reflected on a particular company policy in relation to a certain ethical standard, an ongoing customer was lost, and quite possibly others abandoned the company after hearing how it handled the situation:

> I've been reported for being a customer advocate and saying, "Hey. This customer owes you $20,000. You're going to cut him off and make him lose his business as a carrier. He's got $6,000 cash in his hand. It's Thursday afternoon. He's got a court order from the judge saying that the funds will be available on Monday, and you are going to make that man unemployed. You're going to dismiss fourteen people because of that, and he's got $6,000 cash in his hand and he owes you twenty, and you can't accept that as good faith for three days?" "No, we can't." And they . . . put him out of business."

An important characteristic of critical reflection is that it encompasses the rethinking and/or aligning of work and its implementation for the way it is carried out in relation to organizational goals and strategies. One manager in this study described a team that addressed the open-ended question of what their human resources needs were going to be in the 1990s. The group showed remarkable perspicacity in their inquiry. The company decentralized, located its offices in areas with quality-of-life appeal for employees, and prepared to shrink its labor force. All of these moves ran counter to what the company had done in the past, when it had offered virtually lifetime employment in return for complete loyalty.

Influence of Senior Management

The leadership in this company discouraged informal critical reflection among employees when leadership was intolerant of those who questioned the status quo. This issue is particularly relevant today, because many organizations and their leaders are precariously balanced on a precipice between control and flexibility. The following comments by a midlevel black manager in his mid-thirties illustrates how the company leadership viewed this situation:

> I've always perceived that it's not dangerous to be a questioner. But someone pointed out to me [that] you have to recognize that it depends on . . . who's the person doing the questioning? and . . . what are they questioning about? And his perception was that people from [a particular part of the company] could question more if they were one of the favored, because it was accepted from them.

> When I first started [questioning the company], I went from [a position of significant responsibility] to a director of special projects, where I had no financial responsibility. They gave me the title of director of special projects, but they never had any special projects. So that's the type of punishment that I can say is very specific. They take away your motivation for coming in.

This comment demonstrates that employees need to discern which questions are welcome and which are not. Those that are not welcome threaten someone else's power or sense of control—even if the overall effect on the company might be beneficial.

Another element contributing to whether or not employees ask "hard" questions is the question of rewards. Most of the managers interviewed in this company believed that rewards were sometimes given for what top management claimed was valued and sometimes in direct opposition to those values. When I asked managers what the company rewarded, they repeatedly noted this inconsistency. For example, Bill, a midlevel white manager in his forties, noted, "Intelligence, hard work, innovativeness, and personal risk taking are rewarded. On the other hand, so is loyalty, familiarity with higher-ups, no risk taking, covering your ass, and obsequiousness." Such inconsistency has an impossible-to-ignore effect on how comfortable employees will be with reflecting critically. Marilyn, a lower-level black employee in her mid–twenties, emphatically stated, "I'm a skeptic now . . . and a coward [laughter]. No—I'm more cautious. I don't want to be a skeptic. But there are things that have happened since I've been here that have made me lean that way."

Recognizing that such skepticism may be a pragmatic stance for individuals who want to survive organizational life, the loss of informal learning within the organization may be significant. Such a loss is the outcome when leadership states one thing but acts in a different way. Employees become skeptical, "cowardly," and demoralized, and they learn to keep their learning to themselves. Such a loss of learning in a time when old solutions consistently fail to solve new problems represents a cost that has yet to be measured.

Barriers to Informal Critical Reflection

How can organizations best capture and use informal critically reflective learning by employees? This research identified three key barriers that have to be overcome: internal competition and employees' tendency to protect their turf, conflict avoidance, and actions taken without adequate consideration of the benefits and consequences. The following briefly discusses the implications of each of these barriers.

Internal Competition and Employees' Tendency to Protect Their Turf

Protecting turf and competing internally means that employees and their managers see themselves as individual contributors who are in competition with others in the organization. Although fighting for budget dollars is nothing new, hoarding information is, and it has become increasingly common. In an environment in which critical reflection is important (a fast-moving, global, entrepreneurial environment), a free flow of information is absolutely essential. The following description by an upper-level white manager in his late forties will be familiar to many: "Our implementation now has been centered in a number of people who are politically adept but are now beginning to build fiefdoms, if you will. They want control. They want to be stars. They're intra-competitive as opposed to inter-competitive: competing against each other for turf."

Conflict Avoidance

The pattern of conflict avoidance, in which people revert to "polite" communication, results in a stunning loss of information to organizations and a breakdown in learning systems. In such situations people may be "sitting" on information that is crucial to others in the organization. Donald, an upper-level white manager in his late fifties, shared his sense of how pervasive and intransigent the problem of conflict avoidance is. He stated that the company had tried to develop a culture in which "it's okay to bring issues to the table for resolution, and it is not okay to deal with them around the perimeter." But, he added, "I don't know what it is about us as human beings, but we tend not to want to talk about the most important things to us that are problems." This pattern is apparent in communications among employees about careers, development, and learning goals. Dave, an upper-level white manager in his mid–forties, speaks directly to this: "It's hard, I think, to be honest about that area . . . because I think we have a tendency in this business . . . to kind of dance around that issue, or to just sit back and say, 'Somebody's going to think I'm wonderful,' and make that happen for me, and that's not how it happens really."

Acting Without Adequate Consideration of the Benefits and Consequences

One of the most destructive employee behaviors mentioned by the managers in this study was acting without adequate consideration for the benefits and consequences. Kurt, an upper-level white manager in his early forties, described how he viewed this pattern: "There are times when there is almost a messianic fervor in some of our approaches to things. . . . For instance, the chairman pronounced one day that competition was the only thing that would protect the consumers in the long run and [that] in order to compete we must achieve a particular goal. And bang! It was like somebody stamped the Eleventh Commandment on the tablet. . . . Everybody sallied forth, not knowing what it meant, not knowing what the financial consequences or risks were, not knowing how to do it." Although by the end the company had made substantial progress on a related goal, Kurt continued, it had done little toward achieving its stated goal and had actually created new roadblocks and problems for itself in that area.

Organizations tend to adopt management fads and their accompanying external consultants without always considering the consequences. This leads to disillusionment and cynicism, a loss of time and money, and little lasting benefit. Without critical reflection, organizations may adopt goals, strategies, and tactics that may not fit their needs.

Lessons Learned

Organizations have within their reach multiple ways to develop critically reflective employees, and many of these can come at little or no expense. Virtually every strategy for developing these employees integrates the educational process with the work employees must do, thus virtually eliminating the age-old problem of training: how do you transfer what is learned to the world of work?

There are many ways to develop critically reflective learning, including a variety of work experiences, a liberal education, open-ended assignments, modeling, encouragement of questioning, honest feedback, and participation in policymaking and policy implementation. The following paragraphs highlight some of the key strategies in developing reflective learning.

A Variety of Work Experiences

Many of these managers were exposed to different perspectives. They identified different solutions to the same problem and were able to see a situation from other points of view. They learned the subcultures of different parts of the company, the attitudes and styles of different managers, and how to solve the distinct problems presented by particular jobs. Limited experience contributed to narrowness of vision.

Educational Experiences

Educational experiences that helped managers become critically reflective included external courses in liberal arts topics and personal development and internal workshops in consciousness raising and organizational development. These experiences helped managers to consider a situation objectively and within a broad context: they transformed managers' perspectives on issues related to diversity (race, gender, sexuality) and enhanced their awareness and capacity to use alternative patterns of management. Gerald, a white upper-level manager in his late fifties, described how a broad education helped him gain new insights concerning the issue of race: "I'm a lot more willing and able to recognize the things that I do and that people around me do that are really racist. And not that it's okay to be racist, but I shouldn't expect myself not to be. So rather than denying it, I'm saying, 'Okay, what is it I'm doing? Okay, I did it again.' And dealing with it openly."

Open-Ended Assignments

When individuals are told exactly how to carry out an assignment, critical reflection can be stifled. According to several of the managers, the freedom to work according to the dictates of their own judgment allowed them to solve a problem or achieve an objective rather than their having to comply with external expectations just to please the boss.

Modeling

Several managers found that through modeling they learned specific strategies for critical reflection. John, an upper-level white manager in his early sixties, commented specifically on the kind of strategy he employed: "I taught him to do his work for the company as if it were his own business. Have fun with it. Play with it. The critical thing here is that you don't become afraid to make decisions because you're always trying to second-guess your boss, but make decisions as though it were your own business." Additionally, more than one individual believed he or she was helped by being given the opportunity to help someone at the upper levels of the organization.

Practice in Critical Questioning

No cognitive ability or skill can be developed without practice. For employees to develop the ability to be critically reflective and to use that ability in their work, they need to see others do it, see that it is valued and useful, and try it themselves. Organizations can encourage employees in a number of different ways to develop an ability for critically reflective learning. For example, companies can actively solicit employee participation and divergent opinions; they can reward others for critical questioning; and they can set and maintain a danger-free environment. Richard, an upper-level white manager in his early forties, described the responsibility of an organization's leadership in this: "The leadership has to permit and insist on the time for reflection and the proper environment. If critical reflection is not rewarded or sought, very little of it will take place, because we get so tied up in our day-to-day [activities. Management needs to give] a lot more people the opportunity to [provide] input and then [say] whether the input is diplomatic or not."

Matthew, an upper-level white manager in his early forties, pointed out what is lost when people are afraid to make mistakes or are afraid of political retribution: "If you create an environment in which people only report everything that they've absolutely thought out and they're sure it is going to fly politically, you sure miss a lot."

Personal Feedback

Personal feedback can provide individuals with perspectives on themselves that are impossible for them to get in any other way. The most profound learning is that which we most vigorously resist. Matthew, an upper-level white manager in his early forties, speaks poignantly to this point:

> When I first started working for [a manager in the company], I thought we were going to kill each other. I mean, we had some absolute knock-down, drag-out types of things, and so finally, in one session, he sat next to me and said, "Look. Let me tell you what I need from you in order for us to get along, and you tell me what you need from me." And he said, "And you can change what I need from you or you cannot." He said, "I'm perfectly willing to live with us not doing that."
>
> And he told me what it was, and it took me awhile, and I did it and was probably better for it. But it was not easy. Because I thought I was absolutely right in what I was doing. I thought what I was doing was absolutely correct. I thought, "Why not? Got me this far. Must be doing something right."

Matthew believed that his manager thought he was a very competent and worthwhile person, but Matthew did not know the extent to which his own behavior was harming his efforts until his manager told him. When people get this kind of feedback, they are pulled in a deeply personal way out of their complex of beliefs. If the message is delivered in such a way that they can really hear it, they begin to entertain the possibility that their relationships are not always what they think.

Participation in Policymaking and Policy Implementation

When people are involved in all levels of policy formation, strategy, and implementation, they are able to see how the process works at each level. In a sense, this process of moving up and down levels of abstraction is somewhat analogous to moving across cultures. The organization perceived by those who make policy is often very different from the organization perceived by those who must implement it.

Looking Forward

Patterns of employee relations can either enhance or inhibit informal critically reflective learning, in that they either positively or negatively affect the flow of information among employees. Poor interpersonal skills are a familiar problem in most organizations and one that is rarely addressed. In organizations that focus on technology, even fewer interpersonal skills are usually brought into the organization, employees have little inclination to develop in this area, and the organization's leaders rarely see the value in emphasizing these skills. However, organizations in which new knowledge development occurs at a rapid pace must be continually ready to question yesterday's truths and to find new ways of doing things. This kind of continuous learning requires a constant movement of information and knowledge. Employees who facilitate rather than impede this movement are essential to informal critical reflection and to success in this environment.

One area where the need for critical reflection is especially apparent is situations characterized by conflict avoidance. Employees and bosses have difficulty putting troublesome issues and problems on the table. One place where conflict avoidance is often particularly evident is in meetings. For example, one person, possibly the team leader, dominates the meeting. No one says anything. During a break or after the meeting, two or three team members complain about the leader's behavior. Everyone returns to the meeting, but no one says anything about this to the team leader. The next time the team meets, two or three of the team members find reasons not to be present. Those who are present sit in an attitude of resistance, saying little. The team leader continues to dominate the team but tries to get others to do the work. Finally, everyone but the team leader knows what the problem with the team is—the team leader (Brooks, 1994).

If we analyze this scenario we can see a loss of learning in several places. First, learning is lost when team members do not contribute their own information or ideas. Second, learning is lost when the information and ideas brought to the table are not allowed to cross-fertilize—to recombine in new and unexpected ways—or do not prompt participants to reflect critically on what they had assumed was the nature of the problem. Third, learning is lost when a team leader fails to recognize that he or she is alienating other team members. Fourth, learning is lost when other team members miss the opportunity to better understand how groups can work together. Fifth, learning is lost when all participants leave the room frustrated and hostile and return to their worksites determined never to work with that person, or on that team, or on that problem again.

The educational activities described by the managers I interviewed sparked a developmental leap among employees, taking them from the ability merely to generalize (what bureaucracies require of their employees) to the ability to reflect critically (which is what is required by organizations that must change and learn). Critical reflection appears to require a more complex way of thinking. Robert Kegan (1994), in his book *In Over Our Heads,* developed a model of what he terms "the orders of consciousness." The fourth and fifth orders include qualities characteristic of critically reflective learning. To understand the significance of this developmental shift in terms of the needs of today's organizations, we must know how Kegan defines the fourth order. For Kegan, the underlying structure of the fourth order is complex systems. Fourth-order thinking is characterized by an understanding of abstract systems (such as a bureaucracy or the stock market), regulation of relationships through rules and policy, and development of the self (or, in the language of learning, of self-directed learning).

The underlying structure of the fifth order is multiple systems. Thus fifth-order thinking is characterized by the ability to understand multiple systems. The self is no longer defined as having an essential center and clear boundaries but as being coconstructed in relationships with others. Thus one's self-concept may include multiple and even apparently conflicting identities. Kegan refers to this understanding of the self as self-transformation, the interpenetration of selves, and interindividuation.

Formal training and development are especially appropriate in a relatively stable and undifferentiated environment. Once we can no longer hide from or deny the rapidity with which our workplaces and home lives are changing, we have to relinquish our search for universal truths others can teach us or we can teach others. The move to understand how we can encourage learning systems that promote rather than discourage informal critical reflection becomes a requirement for mere survival, not to mention success, in the environment many of the world's organizations inhabit today.

References

Brookfield, S. (1987). *Developing critical thinkers.* San Francisco: Jossey-Bass.

Brooks, A. K. (1992). Building learning organizations: The individual-culture interaction. *Human Resource Development Quarterly,* 3(4), 323–336.

Brooks, A. K. (1994). Power and the production of knowledge: Collective team learning in work organizations. *Human Resource Development Quarterly*, 4(3), 213–236.

Fiol, C. M., & Lyles, M. J. (1985). Organizational learning. *Academy of Management Review, 10*(4), 803–813.

Freire, P. (1972). *Cultural action for freedom.* Middlesex, England: Penguin, 1972.

Kegan, R. (1994). *In over our heads: The mental demands of modern life.* Cambridge, MA: Harvard University Press.

Mezirow, J. (1981). A critical theory of adult learning and education. *Adult Education,* 32(1), 3–24.

Sonnenfeld, J. A. (1985). Education at work: Demystifying the magic of training. In R. E. Walton & P. R. Lawrence (Eds.), *HRM trends and challenges.* Boston: Harvard Business School Press.

Tunstall, W. B. (1986). The breakup of the Bell system: A case study in cultural transformation. *California Management Review,* 28(2), 110–124.

Theory and Practice of Informal Learning in the Knowledge Era

Victoria J. Marsick
Marie Volpe
Karen E. Watkins

The Problem and the Solution. Models of informal learning in today's rapidly changing environment have not fully considered how people make meaning of their context as they frame what they need to learn, seek out strategies for informal learning, and evaluate their experiences. Using a framework developed by Bolman and Deal, the authors identify filters that help identify where informal learners in organizations might best focus their attention. Also, they reevaluate a basic model for informal learning in light of information in the studies in this book that point to the importance of context. Finally, they explore overarching lessons learned about supporting informal learning and becoming intentional about learning.

What have we learned about the theory and practice of informal learning? A pervasive theme throughout this book has been how influential the work environment is on the process of informal learning. This appears to be the case whether the work context is intimate, such as for paramedic partners and small family businesses, or large and impersonal, such as in corporations undergoing major changes. What is striking in all of these studies is that neither the size or complexity of the work context nor the magnitude of the changes taking place in the environment make a substantial difference in terms of informal learning. Rather, what appears to be most significant is how individuals in changing or challenging circumstances perceive their work context and how they consequently decide what they need to learn and how they should go about learning in informal ways.

All of the research described in this book appears to support Kurt Lewin's premise (1935) that individual behavior is a function of the interaction between people and their environment. Given that premise, the analysis in this chapter looks at individuals in terms of their reactions to particular changes in various organizational settings. Bolman and Deal's model (1984) for understanding organizational environments is useful here for examining and synthesizing what we have learned about the effects of the organizational environment on people's behavior and, specifically, on how they learn informally.

The Frames of Bolman and Deal

Bolman and Deal identify four major "frames" for studying organizations as entities: the structural frame, the human resources frame, the political frame, and the symbolic frame. Viewing organizations through these frames allows the researcher to concentrate on various aspects of organizational phenomena and exclude others. No frame is better than any other; rather, the frames are like "windows on the world. . . . They help us order the world and decide what action to take" (p. 4). To set in place the context for this analysis, we describe each of Bolman and Deal's frames and analyze its impact on informal learning.

The Structural Frame

The structural frame is predicated on two assumptions. First, the world is rational, and therefore people make decisions logically, based on facts. Second, organizations set goals and build structures to achieve those goals. This approach views the world as certain, stable, predictable, and nonambiguous and organizations as hierarchies or pyramids. Organizational structure encompasses bureaucracy, adherence to chains of command, and allocation of responsibility and is characterized by formal roles, rules, regulations, policies, and goals. Structure connotes that which is analytic, logical, and rational. It focuses on differentiation (specialization) and integration (links), communication and operating systems, and coordinating mechanisms.

What is the structure and focus of informal learning in organizations when viewed through this frame? When the environment is relatively stable and predictable and there are limited external forces driving an organization to make structural changes, the focus of informal learning is also stable and predictable. Through the structural lens, individuals can be seen as helping others to understand "how things are done here." Their focus is on learning and informally sharing information about new approaches to improve already established processes and systems. Learning is defined by the boundaries of an already existing organizational and structural paradigm. Learning is not focused on radical or irrational innovations meant to change or tamper with the structure but on measures intended to enhance the structure and ensure that it is maintained.

The structural frame views conflict as interference with achievement of goals. Conflict should be resolved by those in charge, the "authorities." In this frame, problems are seen to arise because the structure does not fit the situation. Solutions come from some form of reorganization to remedy the structural mismatch. When those in charge implement changes in the structure, this is often viewed as disorienting by individuals. The focus of informal learning, in this case, moves away from helping others understand the environment and how things are done. Individuals now become more isolated as they begin to focus on learning and figuring out for themselves what are the new roles, rules, and regulations and how they will carry out their responsibilities.

As evidenced in the studies in this book, structural changes more often than not are the result of a major downsizing. Loss of personnel through downsizing programs also has an adverse affect on the informal learning of those who remain in the organization. There is, for example, a loss of institutional memory when a lot of people with expertise leave. There are fewer mentors available to foster informal learning. There are fewer people in the organization, but they are doing more work, with the result that there is less time to exchange information and learn informally.

The Human Resources Frame

The underlying assumption of the human resources frame is that people are the most important resource in an organization. This frame recognizes that people have needs, feelings, prejudices, skills, limitations, capacities to learn, and the tendency to want to defend old attitudes and beliefs. The emphasis on the interdependence of people and the organization is reflected in concepts such as organizational democracy and participative management styles. Rather than chains of command, there is a focus on self-management and self-direction. This frame is also characterized by group dynamics, organizational development interventions, and sensitivity training.

What is the structure and focus of informal learning in this frame? The human resources frame views conflict as something that must be resolved by choosing the best of multiple options and maximizing win-win situations. Solutions come from tailoring the organization to meet the needs of its human resources (its people). Thus the focus of informal learning is to help others get what they need psychologically and emotionally, through such things as job enrichment, personal development, and career progression. Just as important, informal learning centers on building a sense of community, even family, within the organization. Colleagues often become friends who are willing and able to share information and new learning.

The use of the human resources frame thrives when structure is stable. If structural changes result in loss of community through downsizing, then individuals may feel threatened (psychologically and emotionally), abandoned, or isolated. A loss of community results in a loss of rapport and interdependence among colleagues and a loss of allegiance to those in charge, who often were perceived as benevolent and caring parents before the downsizing. The survivors of downsizing often feel a loss of trust and loss of loyalty to the organization and its "authorities." Some survivors become introspective. They feel they can no longer actively engage in informal learning with peers and others in the organization. They feel isolated as they struggle to learn how to sort out and reframe their relationship with the organization. As a consequence, they have little information to share, and because of their need to resolve their own internal issues, they may have even less inclination to help others.

The Political Frame

The basic assumptions underlying the political frame are twofold: in a world of scarcity, there will be winners and losers, and most decisions involve resource allocation. Although each person may be rational within his or her individual view of the world, irrationality begins to show up in the system. Agendas become layered so deeply that the system makes no sense.

In the political frame, conflict is a way of life; it is inevitable and something one has to learn to manage. People focus on learning strategies and tactics for prevailing in a conflict but not necessarily for resolving it. Under relatively stable and predictable organizational conditions, political acumen is expected and acquired informally. Learning how to become politically savvy is never discussed formally or publicly in organizations. Individuals learn the nuances of how work gets done and how ideas are brought forward informally by their peers and others. The political frame considers such elements of organizational life as power and influence, social control and coercion, vested interests, coalitions, bargaining and negotiation, and the allocation of scarce resources.

What is the structure and focus of informal learning in this frame? Problems arise in organizations when power is broadly dispersed or unevenly distributed. Restructuring can lead to uneven distribution of power and ambiguity concerning who has it. In such situations, the intensity of political conflict heightens, and it becomes very difficult to get anything done. When individuals perceive new environments as predominantly political, they learn informally how to negotiate in the organization by cautiously developing and testing new strategies. Often their focus is to ensure their own personal survival or success. Those whose vision extends beyond their own circumstances may see opportunities for advancing new ideas and change efforts. However, in a politicized environment people are also careful about what they reveal to others. Sometimes they seek to protect themselves, and sometimes they decide that others may not be ready to hear what they have to say or may not be able to handle certain information appropriately. As a result, information may be held close to the chest, and at times people may even deliberately spread misinformation.

The Symbolic Frame

In the symbolic frame, appearances underlie assumptions. Both the organization and its leaders are judged not so much by what they do as by how they appear. This frame is most applicable in organizations where the goals are unclear or there is ambiguity concerning tasks, roles, and relationships. Bolman and Deal (1984) say that this frame, unlike the others, views the world as ambiguous and uncertain. Given this kind of confusion, the ability to make decisions may be undermined. Alternatively, a visionary leader can take advantage of eroding norms and perceived chaos to advance a new agenda.

Under even stable and predictable conditions—that is, when an organizational structure is in place and human resources needs are being met—individuals still create symbols to reduce ambiguity and increase predictability. The intent of the use of the symbolic frame is to reduce uncertainty and anxiety, to reassure, to entertain, to give security, to provide knowledge, and to impart what Bolman and Deal refer to as propaganda. The symbolic frame considers the roles of myths, symbols, stories, fairy tales, heroes, drama, actors, rituals, rites, ceremonies, humor, play, and metaphors in organizational life.

What is the structure and focus of informal learning in this frame? When the structure of the organization is intact and relatively stable and predictable, people learn to create, support, and continually participate in the organizational drama (that is, the rituals, ceremonies, stories, and so on in the organization). Such activities reduce anxiety. However, when the organizational structure changes, such as through restructuring and downsizing, anxiety grows and organizational symbols and rituals lose their meaning. In this situation, the focus of informal learning shifts to learning how to make meaning and reduce anxiety for oneself, independent of others. Visionary leaders may learn a new, charismatic style of leadership where the focus is on reframing perceptions of reality and on influencing others.

Learning informally through interactions with others can be severely impeded when the environment becomes unstable and unpredictable. Organizational changes often result in a breakdown of informal networks because of the loss of personnel who had served as mentors, role models, and expert guides. Organizational change can also be very threatening to individual employees. People may be less willing or able to share information as they cope with reframing their relationship with the organization. The flow of information can be severely restricted in such situations, or it can flow freely, almost to the point of inundation, but the individual is left on his or her own to make meaning of it. Leaders may not want to be explicit about their intentions, or the situation may call for greater levels of individual capacity to scan and interpret an ambiguous environment. The overriding implication for informal learning is that many individuals learn to be more independent, and they learn what they need in more independent ways.

Implications for Theory

The principal lessons learned from the informal learning experiences recounted in this book have implications for both theory and practice. In the following paragraphs we revisit informal learning in light of these lessons.

Revisiting Informal Learning

A decade ago, Marsick and Watkins (1990) set out to develop a model of informal and incidental learning that would shed light on the dynamics of such learning and help organizations understand how it could be better facilitated. Table 8.1 summarizes the framework they developed. Their model is based on the action science perspective of Argyris and Schön (1978), which in turn has roots in John Dewey's theories (1938) of learning from experience and Kurt Lewin's understanding (1935) of the interactions between individuals and their environment.

Marsick and Watkins's model notes that people learn from their experience when they face a new challenge or problem. This triggers a fresh look at their situation, followed by a search for alternative responses and then action to rectify the problem and an evaluation of the results. Marsick and Watkins specified a simple type of learning from experience, equivalent to what Argyris and Schön (1978) call single-loop learning—that is, learning to change tactics when faced with a mismatch between intentions and outcomes. This level of informal learning calls for reflecting on tactics, but it does not call for a deeper level of critical reflection aimed at understanding underlying values, beliefs, and assumptions. The model suggests that without this deeper learning, which Argyris and Schön (1978) call double-loop learning, errors in perceptions, judgement, and conclusions often occur. In fact, single-loop learning can be dangerous if it simply reinforces past erroneous formulation and diagnosis about a problematic situation.

Based on this logic, Watkins and Marsick refined their model (see Figure 8.1), which they used as a jumping-off point for further thinking about continuous learning in the learning organization (Marsick & Watkins, 1997; Watkins & Marsick, 1993). The model in Figure 8.1 should not be interpreted as linear or prescriptive. As we have described it elsewhere (Burgoyne & Reynolds, 1997), "steps such as observation and reflection are interwoven throughout various phases of the model, and the learning process varies because of the situation in which people find themselves. The problem-solving cycle is embedded within a sub-surface cycle comprising the beliefs, values and assumptions that guide action at each stage" (p. 297). Because informal and incidental learning is seldom consciously and critically examined, it is subject to a high degree of misinterpretation. People often do not learn from their mistakes; instead, they reinforce their mistakes because they do not examine why they have failed. By subjecting our actions to the lens of critical reflection, we begin to see how beliefs, values, assumptions, contextual factors, and unintended outcomes shape actions and outcomes. Insight into what these factors are can lead to redesign of action, and with practice, to new ways of addressing challenges.

Revising the Model

Attention to the study of informal learning has increased dramatically in the last decade. In her review of the literature, Cseh (1998) found 143 dissertations written between 1980 and 1998 that discussed aspects of informal learning. Cseh found that interpretations of context influenced every step in learning. This lesson is echoed in the "awakening" described by Ziegler in Chapter Six and by the awareness around relationships identified by Lovin in Chapter Three. The first and foremost task of learners was to make sense of the rapidly shifting environment. Cseh describes the impact of context this way (Cseh, Watkins, & Marsick, 1999): "The lenses through which they saw their world framed their critical incidents and learning experiences. The context was sometimes interpreted as a macro level trigger of critical incidents, as a barrier in finding solutions to their problem, or sometimes as offering potential opportunities. Managers described both changes and issues that did not change from the previous regime in their environment and how these impacted their work. As it turned out, neither of these seemed to support and help them in their activities" (p. 354).

Although the context of learning is mentioned in the earlier models, its pervasive influence on every phase of the learning process—as identified by Cseh (1998) and echoed in the chapters in this book—was not that evident. Cseh found that "context permeates every phase of the learning process—from how the learner will understand the situation, to what is

Table 8.1 Marsick and Watkins's Theory of Informal and Incidental Learning

	Informal Learning	*Incidental Learning*
Definitions	Learning that is predominantly experiential and noninstitutional.	Learning that is unintentional, a byproduct of another activity.
Differences from formal learning	Differs by degree of control exercised by the learner, location (not classroom based), and predictability of outcomes.	Differs by degree, since it is a subset of informal learning. It is tacit, taken for granted, and implicit in assumptions and actions.
Examples	Self-directed learning, networking, coaching, mentoring, performance planning, and trial and error.	Learning from mistakes, assumptions, beliefs, attributions, internalized meaning constructions about the action of others, hidden curriculum in formal learning.
	Delimiters of Informal and Incidental Learning	*Enhancers of Informal and Incidental Learning*
Framing	How individuals selected the problems to which they attend and relate them to the context as they explore interpretations.	
Creativity		Different ways of seeing problems and generating solutions.

Proactivity	Process of actively seeking out learning in everyday experiences in various ways.
Critical reflectivity	Taking the time to look deeply at one's practice to identify values, assumptions, and beliefs that govern action.

Source: Adapted from Marsick & Watkins, 1990.

Figure 8.1 Informal and Incidental Learning Model

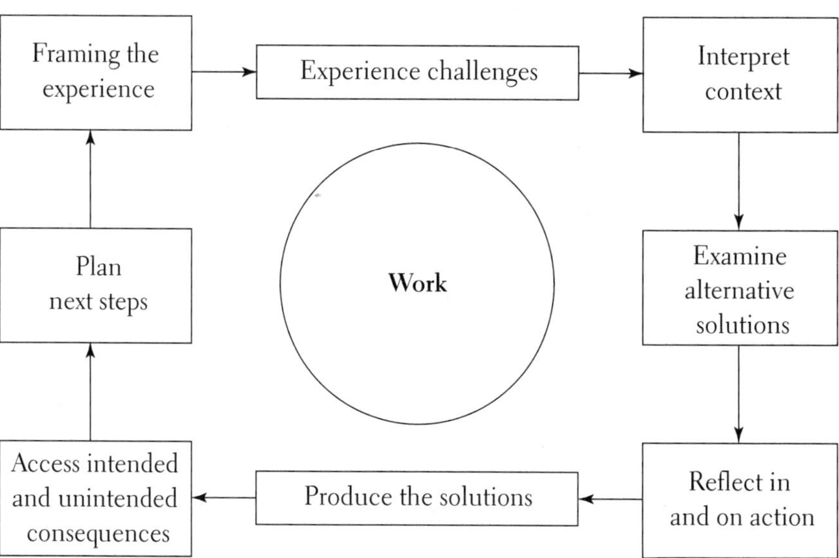

Source: Marsick & Watkins, 1997, p. 299. Reprinted by permission.

learned, what solutions are available and how the existing resources will be used" (Cseh, Watkins, & Marsick, 1999, p. 352). Cseh also found the language used in the earlier models to be too abstract or, at times, not sufficiently descriptive to capture the experience of her participants. Based on these findings, Cseh, Watkins, and Marsick jointly refined the model further, as seen in Figure 8.2. This revised model is attentive to many of the lessons learned from the studies reported in this book.

Implications for Practice

In Chapter One we summarized characteristics of informal learning that have been echoed by all of the chapters of this book:

- It is integrated with work and daily routines.
- It is triggered by an internal or external jolt.
- It is not highly conscious.
- It is often haphazard and is influenced by chance.
- It involves an inductive process of reflection and action.
- It is linked to the learning of others.

Figure 8.2 Reconceptualized Informal and Incidental Learning Model

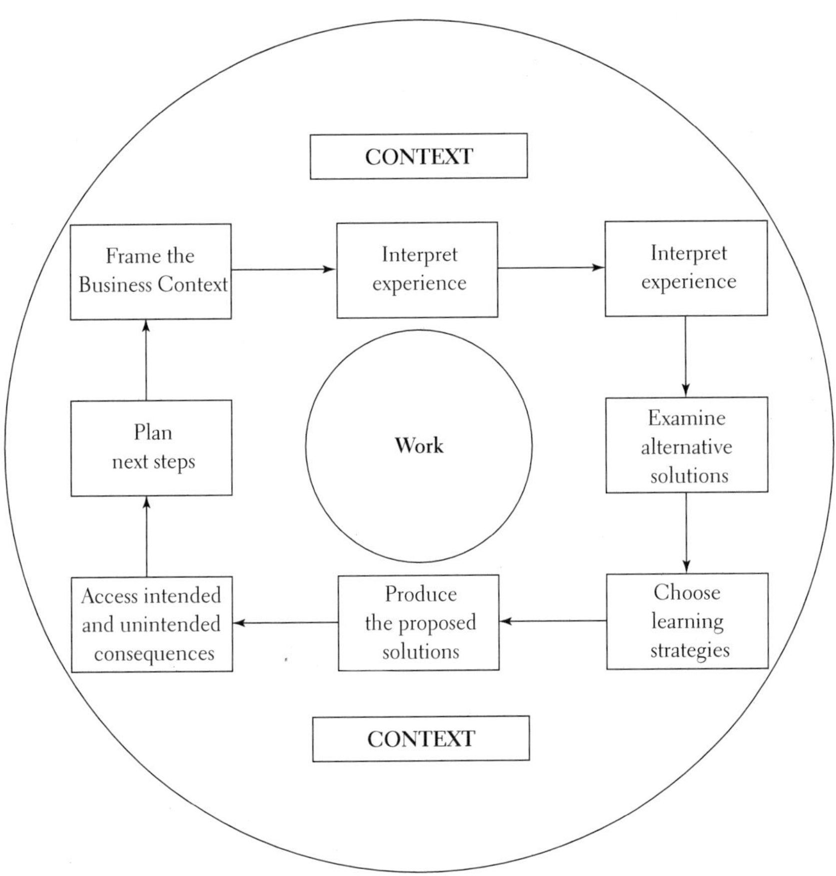

Source: Cseh, Watkins, & Marsick, 1999, p. 354. Reprinted by permission.

From these characteristics we can infer a number of ways to enhance practice:

- Make time and space for learning.
- Scan the environment for changes.
- Pay attention to the learning process.
- Attend to goals and turning points.
- Build an inductive mindset and reflective skills to complement action.
- Build climates of collaboration and trust, or if these are not present, protect oneself when the culture emphasizes distrust.

Each of the chapters in this book has provided specific lessons for practice such as these. Here we draw attention to a few overarching implications for the way in which individuals can enhance their informal learning and the way learning specialists can help them to do this.

Becoming Intentional About Learning

The first step toward enhancing one's own learning is to become more intentional about

- What one wants to learn (learning goals)
- How this learning will help further one's own life or career goals and those of the organization (without assuming that these goals are always congruent)
- How one can best accomplish this kind of learning, given differences in learning styles, personality and motivation variables, and constraints within the organization (for example, systems, rewards, and cultures that are unfriendly to learning, and limited resources)

In Chapter Five Dechant lays out a framework learners can use to jump-start this process. It is predicated on a systems framework that emphasizes enhanced awareness of learning, monitoring of outcomes, and the adjustment of either actions or deeper values and assumptions that have led one to frame these goals as such. Although such self-directed learning sounds easy, it often is not, for reasons internal to the learner or extrinsic in the environment (or both). Many people are not in the habit of continuously learning and may need help developing the skills needed to plan and carry out learning initiatives.

Their awareness of the limitations placed on learning in organizations has led many researchers to develop a keen interest in transformative learning. Jack Mezirow's work (1991) provides a window into how transformative learning occurs. Mezirow's thinking grew out of a study in the 1970s of women who had returned to higher education after raising their families. He discovered that these women were able to reassess fundamental worldviews that had been shaped by society and that they had internalized and accepted uncritically. Mezirow's theory revolves around the realization that adults filter all of their experience through "frames of reference that define their life world." These "structures of assumptions . . . selectively shape and delimit expectations, perceptions, cognition, and feelings . . . [and] set our 'line of action'" (Mezirow, 1997, p. 5). Frames of reference are broad, comprehensive habits of mind that show up in different situations as a point of view that shapes interpretation of a specific event. Frames of reference and points of view can be psychological, political, social, cultural, economic, or epistemological. For example, a trainer who works multiculturally has to constantly confront the frames of mind that he has internalized around gender, race, and class. Frames of mind are reflected in pedagogical choices, such as choice of reading material or learning activities, selection of people to answer questions or to work on particular projects, and even in seating arrangements. Mezirow notes that people can transform their thinking when they can identify and critique the assumptions behind their actions.

There are, as Brooks notes in Chapter 7, many obstacles to engaging in critically reflective learning in organizations. The key challenge is this: although leaders and managers might cognitively recognize the value of deep questioning, they are seldom prepared to truly accept critical challenges to their beliefs or to the organization. Because learning is truly becoming a highly social activity, an increase in individual capacity to challenge beliefs quickly leads to heightened conflict. One clear need is for increased abilities to uncover and address assumptions and beliefs that have often not been laid on the table for public consumption. Imbalances in power relationships often make this kind of challenging difficult and dangerous, however.

Supporting Informal Learning

Organizations have found that informal learning from experience cannot be left completely to chance. Conscious planning can help learners to prioritize and meet learning goals. Organizations often recommend a structured process to help individuals plan for their own learning, which they might tie to performance management, skills development, or job mobility. At the heart of such a process is a form of learning contract. Learning contracts ask that learners identify needs, set learning goals, decide on assessment criteria, and locate appropriate strategies and resources. Learning contracts are used in courses or in independent learning projects. Organizations might identify desired competencies employees can assess themselves against to identify learning gaps. An employee can assess himself or herself against a set of desired capabilities (often on computer) and then follow a planning protocol and access resources for learning—such as workshops, self-learning materials, and suggested mentors and coaches—to develop the necessary skills and knowledge. Organizations might also help people analyze their learning style so they can choose activities that match their strengths and improve their weaknesses.

Such planning does not have to be bureaucratic but can easily become so. Some businesses have been trapped by planning for its own sake. An alternative is a flexible approach to planning that balances bottom-up thinking with a strategic focus from the top. What makes sense, from the institution's view, is the idea of a strategic direction that is expressed in an organizational vision. Individuals have their own visions, too, an idea that Peter Senge (1990) captured in the notion of personal mastery. People become the most they can be when they are driven by their own internal vision. Institutions capitalize on knowledge when they help people align their own contributions more effectively with the institution's strategic intent.

Conclusion

Informal learning is playing an increasingly central role in the lives of individuals and the agendas of organizations. Informal learning is not a substitute for structured training or education. Often, learning is much more productive if it is designed, planned, and facilitated in some way. However, the evidence suggests that the need for more effective informal learning from experience is also rising.

One final caveat. Various authors have noted that the interests of the organization and those of the individual are not always complementary and that organizations inevitably have the upper hand when it comes to power and authority to make decisions. We do not want to seem naïve about these issues. We do recognize that organizations may exploit individuals, although we also argue that they do not always do so. Remember, "the organization" is simply a group of people, and people can be negotiated with. The individual often does need to negotiate his or her relationships with people who hold power, and the deck may indeed be stacked in favor of those individuals. Nonetheless, those with a greater capability for learning can assume more authority in these relationships. When circumstances are favorable and people in power are open to negotiation, learning-enabled people will achieve more of what they want, both for themselves and for the groups, institutions, and organizations to which they belong. And when circumstances are not favorable, skilled learners can use their skills for their own benefit and protection.

References

Argyris, C., & Schön, D. (1978). *Organizational learning: A theory of action perspective.* Reading, MA: Addison-Wesley.

Bolman, L. G., & Deal, T. E. (1984). *Modern approaches to understanding and managing organizations.* San Francisco: Jossey-Bass.

Burgoyne, J., & Reynolds, M. (Eds.). (1997). *Management learning: Integrating perspectives in theory and practice.* Newbury Park, CA: Sage.

Cseh, M. (1998). *Managerial learning in the transition to a free market economy in Romanian private companies.* Unpublished doctoral dissertation, The University of Georgia, Athens.

Cseh, M., Watkins, K. E., & Marsick, V. J. (1999, March). Re-conceptualizing Marsick and Watkins' model of informal and incidental learning in the workplace. In K. P. Kuchinke (Ed.), *Proceedings, Academy of Human Resource Development Conference, Volume I* (pp. 349–356), Baton Rouge, LA: Academy of Human Resource Development.

Dewey, J. (1938). *Experience and education.* New York: Macmillan.

Lewin, K. (1935). *A dynamic theory of personality.* New York: McGraw-Hill.

Marsick, V. J., & Watkins, K. E. (1990). *Informal and incidental learning in the workplace.* London: Routledge.

Marsick, V. J., & Watkins, K. E. (1997). Lessons from informal and incidental learning. In J. Burgoyne & M. Reynolds (Eds.), *Management learning: Integrating perspectives in theory and practice* (pp. 295–311). Newbury Park, CA: Sage.

Mezirow, J. (1991). *Transformative dimensions of adult learning.* San Francisco: Jossey-Bass.

Mezirow, J. D. (1997). Transformative learning: Theory to practice. In P. Cranton (Ed.), *Transformative learning in action: Insights from practice* (New Directions in Adult and Continuing Education, No. 79, pp. 5–12). San Francisco: Jossey-Bass.

Senge, P. M. (1990). *The fifth discipline: The art and practice of the learning organization.* New York: Doubleday.

Watkins, K. E., & Marsick, V. J. (1993). *Sculpting the learning organization: Lessons in the art and science of systemic change.* San Francisco: Jossey-Bass.

Design of Studies

Victoria J. Marsick

The studies reported in this book were all interpretive case studies based on collecting and analyzing qualitative data. The researchers relied especially on open-ended interviews, using interview protocols they designed and field tested before beginning their research. Researchers typically triangulated interview data with written critical incidents, nonparticipant observation, or document analysis. They collected demographic and background information so that they could describe the degree to which their samples were representative of the larger population. They also analyzed their data for patterns that might be affected by characteristics of their samples.

Samples were typically convenience samples—that is, people who were in the organization that the researcher studied; met designated criteria regarding characteristics, such as the types of work they were doing, their function, or their experience; and, in some cases, were identified as a good example of the phenomenon being described. The samples were thus biased in favor of the characteristics the researchers wanted to describe. The researchers deliberately tried to find people who were likely to be informal learners, so that they could better describe such learning in context and identify the conditions in the environment that might influence their learning patterns. Sample size ranged from twenty to thirty people.

Data Collection and Analysis

Data were typically collected over a period ranging from three to six months. Research instruments for many of these studies were designed, initially, to probe factors such as the following (Marsick and Watkins, 1987, p. 178):

1. Context: trigger events and relationships to life transitions and factors inside and outside the workplace
2. Nature of learning: problematic situations, needs, interests, and objectives and whether or not learning fell primarily in one or another of the learning domains
3. How, when, and from whom the learning originated
4. Learning processes, strategies, and techniques
5. Consequences of learning
6. Degree and nature of awareness of taken-for-granted assumptions: norms and their impact on action as well as reframing of problems or situations, if this occurred
7. Feelings about the learning situation, both immediate and later

Researchers also typically collected data about the setting so that they could understand the organization as a learning system and the way in which factors in the environment might facilitate or impede learning. For example, studies looked at the organization's culture as well as at the way learning might have been affected by structure, systems, leadership, and policies or practices.

Data were analyzed inductively using a constant comparative method of content analysis. Elements of grounded theory (Glaser & Strauss, 1967; Strauss & Corbin, 1990) were used to guide analysis. Researchers started with a conceptual framework that they based on the literature and that typically revolved around work by Jack Mezirow (1991) on transformative learning. That framework is discussed later in the appendix. This framework guided their initial analysis, but researchers often found that they needed to modify or abandon it because it did not adequately tell the story in the data.

Working with colleagues, researchers began their analysis with open coding that was sensitive to the researcher's focus and the conceptual framework. Researchers also sought out unanticipated themes expressed in the language of the participants. Sometimes the original conceptual framework identified by the researcher was completely changed, because it did not tell the story found in the data (as was the case for Marie Volpe and Ann Brooks). At other times, elements of the framework worked but were significantly modified or built on because of unique properties in the population or the environment, as was the case for Barbara Lovin. Once a coding scheme was created, several analysts coded the same set of interviews and reconciled different interpretations to establish inter-rater reliability.

As data were analyzed using a finalized coding scheme, researchers typically constructed matrices to synthesize data and to analyze segments of the data in relationship to a particular construct.

The Conceptual Framework

Many of the studies in this book were based on the notion that people might learn different things, and do so through different strategies, depending on the type of learning that they are doing. They drew on the conceptual framework in Figure A.1, which came out of discussions among Jack Mezirow, Stephen Brookfield, and Victoria Marsick around the nature of informal learning (Marsick & Watkins, 1987). The distinctions are drawn from Mezirow's early conceptualization of three different domains of learning (1991), which he in turn based on the communication theories of Jürgen Habermas (1984, 1987). (Mezirow subsequently refined his thinking to suggest that there are two basic learning domains: instrumental and communicative learning. Emancipatory learning can take place in either domain.) The three domains of learning are instrumental, communicative, and self-reflective learning. Instrumental learning focuses on task-oriented problem solving. Communicative learning focuses on the way in which people come to understand and agree on consensual norms in their societies. Self-reflective learning refers to the way in which people understand and manage themselves in the world.

Mezirow's (1997) theory revolves around the realization that adults filter all of their experience through "frames of reference that define their life world." These "structures of assumptions . . . selectively shape and delimit expectations, perceptions, cognition, and feelings . . . [and] set our 'line of action'" (p. 5). Frames of reference are broad, comprehensive habits of mind that show up in different situations as points of view that shape interpretations of specific events. Frames of reference and points of view can be psychological, political, social, cultural, economic, or epistemological. For example, a trainer who works multiculturally has to constantly confront the frames of mind that he has internalized around gender, race, and class. Frames of mind are reflected in pedagogical choices, such as the choice of reading material or learning activities, ways in which people are drawn into conversations in training sessions, or what is or is not open for discussion.

▲ Figure A.1 Initial Conceptual Framework for Studies of Informal Learning

Learning About the Job
- Productivity

Learning About the Organization
- Commitment, job satisfaction
- Team relationships, including networking, coaching, mentoring, role modeling; power and politics; status
- Philosophy, mission, and goals; roles; rules and how they are interpreted, negotiated, and modified

Learning About Oneself
- Confidence building or undermining
- Competence building or undermining
- Identification with the organization
- Dealing with authority
- Coping with unfair treatment, rejection, ambiguity, failure, or competition
- Coping with personal tragedy
- Progress within organization
- Changes in values, belief system, or self-concept
- Dealing with discrepancies between personal values and those of the organization
- Changes in orientation toward the job, the organization, or one's career or role

Source: Marsick & Watkins, 1987, p. 177.

Mezirow concludes that people can transform their thinking when they can identify and critique the assumptions behind their actions. Mezirow's theory emphasizes rational discourse, and as such it has come under fire for being excessively cognitive. He does not exclude the role of emotions, but he also does not fully elaborate the constructive role emotions can take in learning under a holistic framework. Transformative education is not simply a cognitive version of sharing thoughts and feelings in a fairly uncritical fashion, as some views on facilitation may advocate. Transformative learners identify different viewpoints, draw on imagination and metaphor, assess reasons and evidence, experiment, and explore feelings.

Instrumental learning (learning about the job) commonly occurs when people learn how to do their job better. It is thus frequently the focus of skills and competency development in organizations. People identify a problem, formulate a hypothetical course of action, try it out, observe the consequences, and assess the results. Learning in this domain is described as fairly prescriptive, because there often is a right way of doing things based on many years of experience. Communicative learning (learning about the organization) takes place in work settings in which people learn about the culture of the organization or when they interpret policies, procedures, visions, missions, strategy statements, goals, and objectives. This kind of learning is aimed at increased understanding of the situation. Self-reflective learning (learning about the self) is directed at personal change and self-management. Change in this domain could involve single-loop or double-loop learning. As the studies in this book show, it is difficult to separate out instrumental, communicative, and self-reflective learning in practice, even though it is possible to think about them differently in theory.

References

Glaser, B., & Strauss, A. (1967). *The discovery of grounded theory: Strategies for qualitative research.* Chicago: Aldine.

Marsick, V. J., & Watkins, L. (1987). *Learning in the workplace.* Beckenham, England: Croom- Helm.

Mezirow, J. (1991). *Transformative dimensions of adult learning.* San Francisco: Jossey-Bass.

Mezirow, J. (1997). Transformative learning: Theory to practice. In P. Cranton (Ed.), *Transformative learning in action: Insights from practice.* New Directions in Adult and Continuing Education, No. 79 (pp. 5–12). San Francisco: Jossey-Bass.

Strauss, A., & Corbin, J. (1990). *Basics of qualitative research: Grounded theory procedures and techniques.* Thousand Oaks, CA: Sage.

Strauss, A., & Corbin, J. (1994). Grounded theory methodology: An overview. In N. K. Denzin and Y. S. Lincoln (Eds.), *Handbook of qualitative research* (pp. 273–285). Thousand Oaks, CA: Sage.

Index

A

Additive partnerships, 24–25. *See also* Partnerships

American Telephone and Telegraph (AT&T), 66

Antagonistic Partnerships, 25–26. *See also* Partnerships

Argyris, C., 9, 27, 31, 61, 65, 86, 95

AT&T. *See* American Telephone and Telegraph

Awakening, 53–55, 60–61, 64. *See also* Learning organizations, development of

B

Bandura, A., 9

Barer-Stein, T., 31

Behavior: Lewin's theory of, 13; translation of insight and new thinking into, 58–60

Bolman, L. G., 13, 14, 21, 80, 81, 84, 85, 95

Boydel, T., 53, 65

Brockett, R. G., 44–45, 50

Brookfield, S., 67, 68, 78, 98

Brooks, A. K., 66, 67, 77, 78–79, 93, 97

Brown, J. S., 46, 50

Burgoyne, J., 53, 65, 86–87, 95

Business, small. *See* Learning organizations

C

Candy, P. C., 8, 9

Center for Workforce Development, 4, 9

Certainty, versus discovery, 65

Coaches, 18

Collective learning, from individual learning to, 61–62. *See also* Learning organizations, development of

College of Benefits Knowledge, 18

Communication system, effective, in the workplace, 40

Competition, internal, 72

Conflict avoidance, 72–73

Consciousness, orders of (Kegan), 78

Copeland, L., 33, 41

Corbin, J., 97, 100

Critical questioning, 68–69, 75

Critical reflection: acting without, 73; barriers to, 71–73; and conflict avoidance, 72–73; and critical questioning, 68–69; development of, 73–76; functions of, 69–70; influence of senior management on, 70–71; and internal competition, 72; and orders of consciousness, 78; as response to organizational disruption, 66–78

Critically reflective employees: and critical questioning practice, 75; and educational experience, 74; and modeling, 75; and open-ended assignments, 74–75; and participation in policymaking and implementation, 76; and personal feedback, 75–76; and variety of work experience, 74

Critically reflective learning. *See* Critical reflection

Cseh, M., 91, 95

D

Deal, T. E., 13, 14, 21, 80, 81, 84, 85, 95
Dechant, K., 42, 46, 50–51, 92
Decision-making theory (Simon), 30
Dewey, J., 60–61, 65, 86, 95
Discovery, certainty versus, 65
Double-loop learning (Argyris and Schön), 86. *See also* Informal learning, theories of
Downsized environment: business models, before and after, 13; common perceptions among workers in, 13–14; heartbroken perspective in, 15; human resource (HR) professionals in, 12–20; and increased stress, 18–19; informal learning in, 10–21; learning needs in, 14–16; and loss of formal networks, 17–18; and loss of informal networks, 16–17; and mechanisms for learning, 18; and mentors and coaches, 18; research base for study of, 13; self-defined perspective in, 14–15; survivalist perspective in, 15–16

E

Education, 74, 77–78
Effective leadership. *See* Leadership, effective
Everett, J., 33, 41
Experience, learning from, 49–50

F

Fifth-order thinking (Kagen), 78
Fiol, C. M., 67, 79
Formal networks, loss of, in downsized environment, 17–18
Fortune magazine, 1
Fourth-order thinking (Kegan), 78
Frames, in study of organizations: and human resources frame, 82–83; and political frame, 83–84; and structural frame, 81–82. *See also* Informal learning, theory of
Frames of reference (Mezirow), 92–93, 98–99
Friere, P., 67, 68, 79

G

Glaser, B., 97, 100

H

Habermas, J., 98
Hiemestra, R., 44–45, 50
Human resource (HR) professionals, 12–20
Human resources, as frame for organizational study, 82–83

I

In Over Our Heads (Kegan), 78
Incidental learning (Warnick and Watkins), 87–88
Individual learning, versus collective learning, 61–62
Informal learning: breakdown of, in downsized environment, 16–19; conclusions about the nature of, 3–9; continuous nature of, 12; after downsizing, 10–21; formal learning versus, 3; implications for theory of, 86–89; and intentionality, 92–93; Marsick and Watkins's theory of, 86–89, 90; nature of and need for, 1–9; revised model for, 89–92; support for, 93–94
Informal learning, theories of: and Bolman and Deal's frames, 81–85; and Marsick and Watkins's informal and incidental learning, 86–91; and reconceptualized informal and incidental learning model, 91

Informal learning processes: challenging mental models in, 56–57; learning how to do things differently in, 57–58; making meaning in, 55–56
Insight, 58–60. *See also* Awakening
Instrumental learning, 100
Intentionality, 92–93
Internal competition, 72

J

Jacobs, R. C., 33, 41
Jarvis, P., 49–50, 51, 61, 65
Jelenick, M., 61, 65

K

Kefalas, A. G., 46, 51
Kegan, R., 78, 79
Kolb, D., 45, 51, 65

L

Langer, E., 48, 51
Larson, B. K., 23, 32. *See also* Lovin, B. K.
Leadership, effective, 36–38
Learners: goals of, in downsized environment, 18; three types of, in downsized environment, 14–16
Learning: and collective learning, 61–62; formal versus informal, 3; informal personal strategies for, 35–36; and learning needs among human resources professionals, 20; mechanisms for, 18; within partnerships, 29; partnerships versus tasks as catalysts for, 27–29; strategic mindset for, 45; training versus, 2
Learning organizations, development of: and awakening, 53–55, 60–61; and conscious reflection, 60–61; definition of, 53; factors in, 64; and informal learning, 55–58; moving from individual learning to collective learning in, 61–62; and transformation of insight and new thinking into behavior, 58–60
Lewin, K., 13, 21, 81, 86, 95
Louis, M. R., 46, 51
Lovin, B. K. (Larson), 22, 89, 97
Lyles, M. J., 67, 79

M

Management: and learning in the knowledge era, 42–50; nature of, 57–58; and systems approach, 46, 48
Marsick, V. J., 1, 3, 9, 27, 30, 32, 41, 53, 65, 80, 86–91, 95–97, 98–100
Martin, J., 43
Meaning, making, 55–56. *See also* Informal learning processes
Mental models, challenging, 56–57. *See also* Informal learning processes
Mentors, 18
Metaphor, use of, 55
Mezirow, J., 67, 68, 79, 92, 93, 95, 97–100
Mills, G. E., 33, 41
Modeling, 74

N

Networks: loss of formal, 17–18; loss of informal, 16–17
Nonaka, I., 6, 9

O

Open-systems framework, 45–46
Organizations: brain drain in, 17–18; four-frame approach (Bolman and Deal) to analysis of, 13; and on-the-job informal learning, 20–21

P

Pace, R. W., 33, 41
Palphs, L., 33, 41

Partnerships: additive type of, 24–25; antagonistic type of, 25–26; as catalysts to learning, 27–29; and learning to be a partner, 27; learning within, 29; potentiated type of, 23–24; and responses to job experiences by paramedic partners, 30; synergistic types of, 25–26; types of, 23–26
Pedler, M., 53, 65
Personal feedback, 75–76
Personal learning strategies, informal, 35–36
Personal mastery (Senge), notion of, 94
Policymaking, 76
Political frame for organizational study, 83–84
Potentiated partnerships, 23–24. *See also* Partnerships
Practice, transforming informal learning theory into, 90–92
Process, linking strategy to, 45–48

R

Reflection: definition of, 60–61; process of, 7
Restructuring. *See* Downsized environment
Reynolds, M., 86, 95

S

Schoderbek, C. G., 46, 51
Schoderbek, P. P., 46, 51
Schön, D. A., 27, 29, 31, 32, 61, 65, 86, 95
Self-directed learning (SDL): and effective management, 50; and learning from experience, 44–48; open systems framework for, 45–48; strategic mindset for, 45; systems approach to, 44–48; systems view of, 47; three-part definition for, 44
Self-reflective learning, 100
Senge, P. M., 2, 9, 53, 56, 61, 65, 94, 95
Senior management, influence of, on critical reflection, 70–71
Sense-making process, 46–48
Shrivastava, P., 61, 65
Simon, H. A., 30, 32
Single-loop learning (Argyris and Schön), 86
Social contract, implied, 12
Sonnenfield, J. A., 67, 79
Stata, R., 61, 65
Stephans, E., 33, 41
Sterman, J. D., 61, 65
Strategy: linking, to process, 45–48; and strategic mindset, 45; for team membership, 34–36
Strauss, A., 97, 100
Stress, increase in, 189
Structural frame for organizational study, 81–82
Supervision, nature of, 57–58
Symbolic frame for organizational study, 84–86
Synergistic partnerships, 26. *See also* Partnerships
Systems approach, for self-directed learning (SDL), 45–48

T

Takeuchi, H., 9
Tasks, as catalysts for learning, 27–29
Team meetings, well-designed agendas for, 40
Team membership: and ability to work as part of team, 33; barriers to, 38; conclusions about, 38–41; and effective leadership, 36–37; and efficient operational structure, 37;

and facilitators of learning effective team membership, 36–38; and individual facilitators, 38; and informal personal learning strategies, 35–36; and management personnel, 39; strategies for, 34–36; and structured on-the-job training, 34; study of, 33–41; and team focus, 37
Training: versus learning, 2; on-the-job, as strategy for learning effective team membership, 34
Tunstall, W. B., 66, 79

V

Velk, R., 45
Vernon, S., 33
Volpe, M., 1, 10, 80, 97

W

Watkins, K. E., 3, 9, 27, 30, 32, 33, 41, 53, 65, 86–91, 95–97, 98–100
Weick, K., 48, 50, 51
Worker inquiry, commitment to facilitation of, 41
Workplace: effective communication in, 40; and informal workplace learning, 4; and informated workplace, 2
Workplace learning: effective facilitation of, 37; and individual facilitation, 38; and interrelational facilitation, 37

Z

Ziegler, M., 52, 89
Zuboff, S., 2, 9

Ann K. Brooks is associate professor of adult education and human resource development at the University of Texas at Austin, where she also codirects the Masters of Human Resource Development Leadership Program. She received her Ed.D. in adult and higher education from Columbia University. Her major areas of teaching and research are adult and organizational learning, women's development, and qualitative and action research.

Kathleen Dechant is a faculty member at the University of Connecticut Business School, Stamford Campus. She received her Ed.D. from Columbia University. Prior to her academic appointment in 1988, she was vice president of employee development at The Equitable Companies. Her research and publications focus on team and organizational learning, diversity, and group knowledge management in virtual environments.

Barbara Keelor (Larson) Lovin is associate professor and head of the Department of Health Sciences at Western Carolina University. She has spent the past twenty-three years teaching emergency medicine to paramedics in degree programs and continuing professional education seminars. Her interest in learning partnerships grew out of her experiences as a practicing paramedic. Keelor-Lovin earned her doctoral degree from Columbia University.

Victoria J. Marsick is professor of adult and organizational learning in the Department of Organization and Leadership at Columbia University, where she also directs graduate programs in adult education. Marsick received her Ph.D. in adult education from the University of California, Berkeley, and an M.P.A. in international public administration from Syracuse University. She consults with both the public and private sectors on learning organizations and on action learning. Marsick served as coeditor of this issue.

Sally Vernon is an educational consultant who works with public schools, universities and colleges, nonprofit organizations, and corporations to develop and implement educational programs that result in individual, group, and organizational change. Products of these collaborations include short-term training programs, workshops and seminars, and certification programs. Vernon received her bachelor and masters degrees from DePaul University and her doctoral degree from Columbia University.

Marie Volpe is adjunct professor of adult and organizational learning at Columbia University, where she teaches graduate classes in staff development and training. Volpe received her doctorate in adult education and masters in organizational psychology from Columbia University. She retired from a thirty-year career at Exxon Corporation, where she held numerous domestic and overseas assignments. Volpe served as coeditor of this issue.

Karen E. Watkins is professor of human resource development at the University of Georgia, where she is director of the HRD graduate program. Watkins's research and consulting interests are in the areas of organizational and action learning. She received her Ph.D. from the University of Wisconsin-Madison and is a past president of the Academy of Human Resource Development.

Mary Ziegler is director of the Center for Literacy Studies at the University of Tennessee in Knoxville. The Center's mission is to conduct research and provide professional development in adult learning and literacy. Her current research activities include a study on the ways practitioners integrate literacy skills and work-related skills to increase employability. Ziegler received her doctorate from Columbia University.

Using *Advances in Developing Human Resources* as a Text

The size and style of each issue of *Advances* makes it perfect for use as a text for short courses and workshops, and as a supplemental text for graduate and undergraduate courses. I encourage you to consider using *Advances* in your teaching. For example, we are using issues 1 and 2 as supplemental texts at the University of Minnesota. These two monographs introduce our students to important ideas from fourteen HRD scholars.

We are using *Advances* issue #2—"Action Learning: Successful Strategies for Individual, Team, and Organizational Development" edited by Yorks, O'Neil, and Marsick—as a supplementary text in our Personnel Training and Development course. The primary texts are *Analysis for Improving Performance: Tools for Diagnosing and Documenting Workplace Expertise* by Swanson and *Structured On-the-Job Training: Unleashing Employee Expertise in the Workplace* by Jacobs and Jones.

For our Strategic Planning in HRD course, we are using *Advances* issue #1—"Performance Improvement Theory and Practice" edited by Torraco—as a supplementary text. The primary text is *Improving Performance: Managing the White Space in Organizations* by Rummler and Brache, along with other readings on strategy, scenario building, systems thinking, and quality.

Anyone interested in the syllabi for these two courses should send me an e-mail at swanson2@cris.com. I would also like to hear from you how you are using the *Advances* monographs.

Richard A. Swanson
Editor-in-Chief

Academy of Human Resource Development

The Academy of Human Resource Development (AHRD) is a global organization made up of, governed by, and created for the human resource development (HRD) scholarly community of academics and reflective practitioners. The Academy was formed to encourage systematic study of human resource development theories, processes, and practices; to disseminate information about HRD; to encourage the application of HRD research findings; and to provide opportunities for social interaction among individuals with scholarly and professional interests in HRD from multiple disciplines and from across the globe.

AHRD membership includes a subscription to *Advances in Developing Human Resources, Human Resource Development Quarterly*, and *Human Resource Development International.* A partial list of other benefits includes (1) membership in the only global organization dedicated to advancing the HRD profession through research, (2) annual research conference with full proceedings of research papers (900 pages), (3) reduced prices on professional books, (4) subscription to the *Forum,* the academy newsletter, and (5) research partnering, funding, and publishing opportunities. Senior practitioners are encouraged to join AHRD's Global 100!

Academy of Human Resource Development
P.O. Box 25113
Baton Rouge, LA 70894-511
USA

Phone: 225-334-1874
Fax: 225-334-1875
E-mail: office@ahrd.org
Website: http://www.ahrd.org

Results

How to Assess Performance, Learning, and Perceptions in Organizations

Richard A. Swanson and Elwood F. Holton III

- Shows human resource development (HRD) professionals how to measure organizational results within the domains of performance, learning, and perceptions
- The widely praised Results Assessment System simplifies the complex issues of assessment, enabling HRD professionals to clearly demonstrate their results
- From the author of *Analysis for Improving Performance,* winner of the Outstanding Instructional Communication Award from the International Society for Performance Improvement and the Society for Human Resource Management Book Award

Results presents a practical guide to building a successful, competitive, and cost-effective HRD practice that meets customers' needs. It teaches a highly effective, easy-to-learn, field-tested system for assessing organization results within three domains: performance (system and financial), learning (knowledge and expertise), and perceptions (participant and stakeholder).

Why measure results in HRD? Because the "corporate school" and "human relations" models of HRD practice, whereby development occurs simply because it is good for employees, no longer works. If HRD is to be a core organizational process, it must hold itself accountable. Measuring results, particularly bottom-line performance, is key to gaining support from top management. And those who measure results ultimately find it a source of program improvement and innovation as well as pride and satisfaction.

Results is both theoretically sound and firmly rooted in practice, offering a core five-step assessment process that gives readers a simple and direct journey from analysis inputs to decision outputs. Whether they have assessment tools but no theory, theory but no tools, or no tools and no theory, this book will equip them to quickly and effectively assess their results.

"*Results* presents the most practical and proven assessment system for the profession"—
Kent Dubbe,
Vice President
of Human Resources,
Longaberger Company

Hardcover, approx.
280 pages
Available April 1999
ISBN 1-57675-004-2 CIP
Item no. 50442-266-602
$34.95

To order call toll-free: **(800) 929-2929**

Internet: www.bkpub.com Fax: 802-864-7627 Or mail to
Berrett-Koehler Publishers, P.O. Box 565, Williston VT 05495

CALL FOR PAPERS

Academy of Human Resource Development

2000 ANNUAL CONFERENCE

Sheraton Imperial Hotel • Raleigh-Durham, NC • March 7–12, 2000

P.O. Box 25113, Baton Rouge, LA 70894 USA, 504-334-1874,
Fax 504-334-1875

The Academy of HRD, an international organization with the mission of encouraging the systematic study of human resource development theories, processes, and practices, encourages you to submit proposals for the 2000 Annual Conference.

All scholars interested in HRD are invited to submit proposals for consideration. The conference is attended by researchers and graduate students in HRD, business, psychology, education, economics, sociology, technology, and communication. In addition, HRD researchers and reflective practitioners from business, industry, and governments participate fully in the conference.

Proposals will be blind reviewed and should consist of new, unpublished research. Papers accepted for the conference program will be published in the conference proceedings and may be published elsewhere following the conference.

Submission Requirements

Authors may submit full manuscripts or proposals. Full manuscripts are strongly encouraged, but abbreviated proposals of 4–5 pages will also be accepted. Manuscripts presenting data-based studies should minimally contain the following elements:

1. Title
2. Problem statement and theoretical framework
3. Research questions and/or hypotheses
4. Methodology
5. Results, conclusions, and limitations
6. Discussion of how this research contributes to new knowledge in HRD

AHRD also welcomes manuscripts presenting new scholarly theory, models, conceptual analyses, literature reviews, and case studies. These papers must also follow the above outline as closely as possible.

Submission Deadlines

Proposals/manuscripts:	*October 1, 1999*
Decision notification:	*November 16, 1999*
Final papers due to proceedings editor:	*January 5, 2000*

Manuscript Requirements

Proposals/manuscripts should meet the following criteria:

1. Typed, double spaced.
2. Should not exceed 20 pages including figures and references (final papers limited to 8 single-spaced pages). Manuscripts that exceed 20 pages will be returned.
3. Blind review ready.
   A. Cover sheet with author(s) identification.
   B. No author identification in body, header, or footer of manuscript.
4. Cover sheet should contain full identification and contact information for *all* authors.
5. All communication with authors will be via e-mail so proposal/manuscript submissions ***must include an e-mail address for all authors***.
6. All deadlines are *firm*. Exceptions will be made only for true emergencies or extraordinary circumstances.
7. All final manuscripts must include a disk copy in MS Word 6.0 (or later) format.

Submission Addresses

Submission by e-mail attachment is strongly preferred. Do not send duplicate manuscripts. If an e-mail submission does not go through, you will be given time to submit a faxed or mailed copy of the manuscript.

E-mail Address

office @ahrd.org

Manuscripts sent as e-mail attachments should specify the word processing format.

Mailing Address

Academy of Human Resource Development
Attn: Conference Chair
P.O. Box 25113
Baton Rouge, LA 70894-5113

Address for Overnight Services

Academy of Human Resource Development
Attn: Conference Chair
Louisiana State University
1142 Old Forestry Building
Baton Route, LA 70803